the art & practice of
trust

THE WAY OF DISCOVERY
Finding Your Way Through Uncertainty, Change & Transition

Victoria Crawford

the art & practice of trust

Copyright © 2009 by Victoria Crawford

All rights reserved. No part of this book may be reproduced or transmitted in any form or by any means, electronically or mechanically, including photocopying or recording without the permission of the author.

Published by Way of Discovery Press.
Book Cover design by Laureen Maurer at Absolute Graphics

ISBN # 978-06-1522-913-3

Printed in the United States of America

Victoria Crawford LLC
Phoenix, AZ
602-870-0060
Victoria@wayofdiscovery.com
www.wayofdiscovery.com

Edition: 1 2 **3** 4 5 6 7 8 9

This book is dedicated with
deep love and gratitude
to my parents
Jeannette and Leland S. Brown Jr.
and to my three children
Sarah, Brian and Jeff Crawford

the art & practice of trust

*"To find the way, close your eyes, listen closely,
and attend with your heart."*
anonymous

the art & practice of trust

Contents

Intention 1
Introduction. 3
CHAPTER ONE
It's about Trust. 5
CHAPTER TWO
Remembering ~ Forgetting. 9
CHAPTER THREE
Overview of the Way of Discovery 15
CHAPTER FOUR
Willingness. 19
CHAPTER FIVE
Awareness. 39
CHAPTER SIX
Discernment. 57
CHAPTER SEVEN
Action. 79
CHAPTER EIGHT
A Final Note 103
CHAPTER NINE
Practices for the Four Quadrants. 105
Acknowledgments 145
About the Author 149
References 151

the art & practice of trust

The Intention

The Art and Practice of Trust offers a pathway, a map of sorts, that will help you find your way through uncertainty, change and transition with a greater sense of creativity, ease and flow. This pathway is called The Way of Discovery.

The intent of this book is to use The Way of Discovery pathway to build and strengthen Self trust. It will help you move your ego, or adapted self, out of the way so that you can connect with your greatest truth and find the answers you seek.

I believe that in order to have the trust that we desire among each other, Self trust is at the foundation of all trust. Our ability, as an individual, to be open, be willing to suspend judgment, listen to our deepest wisdom and act on it, is the source of our true confidence and power. In interaction with others, this inner relationship gives us the freedom to be vulnerable and have the necessary and real conversations so that we can focus on what is most needed and do the work at hand.

The pathway and book came from my desire to share what I have learned: that when we trust our own wisdom and act on its promptings, it will guide us through uncertainty in a way that supports our greatest good, the good of others and helps us realize our greatest potential.

The content of this book comes from my own life experiences, working with clients, reading books, journaling, listening to wise teachers and using what resonated with me in my own life to test its validity.

I encourage you to approach this pathway as a journey of discovery and I welcome you to The Art and Practice of Trust!

Introduction

To have the foundation beneath you disappear or suddenly discover that you can no longer depend on someone or something for security or meaning can be a great difficulty; a crisis.

I am familiar with this territory both in my own life and through my work as a guide and personal coach. I have watched people face uncertainty, loss and betrayal and shift from a state of despair to hope. I have seen long held resentments released and replaced with forgiveness. And I have seen individuals let go of self doubt and worry and take action boldly, with confidence. The common thread for each has been the willingness to take the inner journey, deepen self awareness and trust their inner wisdom.

What I have learned is that times of crisis are also times of discovery. In the midst of uncertainty and unknown, even when the odds seem insurmountable, we can discover that as we trust our Self and act on our inner promptings, we are well led.

Many of us have moved away from this relationship, and it is easy to understand why. So much of life conspires against it. There are many distractions and much that keeps us from the quiet and silence required to turn our attention within and listen to our own wisdom. Consequently, this relationship is often ignored or put aside. When we want truth, it's hard to find and instead fear, worry or confusion can overwhelm and pull us into downward spirals. We forget that we have within us the answers we seek. Fortunately, it doesn't matter how distant this inner connection may feel, it is always there, always present and always available to us regardless of age or depth of struggle, if we are willing to seek it.

In the book, I define Self as that part, within each one of us that is connected to the Source of life; however it is that you define it. For some, it will be found through a faith tradition; for others, it may be simply nature. It is a place of great wisdom, benevolence, love and above all, mystery.

With deep respect and gratitude I offer this work.

CHAPTER ONE

It's About Trust

*If peace comes from seeing the whole,
then misery stems from a loss of perspective*
Mark Nepo

*The real voyage of discovery consists not of seeking
new lands but in seeing with new eyes.*
Marcel Proust

The reason I wrote this book is to share with you a simple pathway to encourage, inspire, and empower you to trust your own wisdom, above all the other voices inside or out, and act on its prompting. This is valuable information to know at any time, but especially helpful during a transition or in a place of uncertainty because when you trust yourself you will know what to do, regardless of the situation you may be facing.

Self trust is at the foundation of confidence, inner peace and bold action. With Self trust you can relax, be present and look for opportunities rather than get caught in fear. It is fear that is underneath worry, confusion, self doubt and overly cautious hesitation that results in lost opportunity and keeps us from doing all that we can and enjoying all that life has to offer.

Who am I to write about this subject? Life could not have chosen a less likely candidate, as I was a person who was filled with self-doubt and routinely looked to others for my answers.

As far back as I can remember, fear was my companion. Life didn't feel safe, and it was not to be trusted. Instead, it was to be figured out, controlled, handled, or hidden from. My inner voice of criticism was much louder than any voice of wisdom or love, so I was easily influenced and doubted my own ability to make good decisions. My view of life, that you had to be vigilant and on guard at all times, made it hard to relax and trust the goodness around me. An unexpected illness, an unwanted divorce, a loss of a job all contributed to a shaky foundation and unease.

"Order is indeed the dream of man, but chaos, which is only another word for dumb, blind, witless chance, is still the law of nature. "
                    Wallace Stegner, Crossing to Safety.

I read this quote years ago, and it haunted me. Was it true? Are we really living our lives amidst chaos where our intentions, hopes, and dreams mean nothing and we are at the mercy of blind chance? Where is God in Stegner's quote? And if not called by that name, at the least, an "order beneath all the disorder" that can guide us through the storms.

My experience has been that there is great uncertainty and unknown in life that can never be fully understood or solved. But I found that there is also a grace in life that can be trusted. I discovered that as I deepened my relationship with my true Self and acted on my inner promptings, it helped me to handle the tension inherent in the uncertainty. I learned how to open up and relax in times when I didn't have answers or was in confusion and discovered the next steps became clear. I found I was consistently led in a way that supported my well-being.

In our world today we are dealing with great uncertainty and unknowns. Economic, environmental, and global challenges, along with the breakdown of trusted institutions, are causing a lot of stress and anxiety. On a personal level, a job loss, illness, divorce, and unexpected or unwanted change can also create great distress. But there is another way. You can become skillful in how to be in the unknown. Rather than trying to avoid what you cannot control, you can learn a new way to relate to it.

To do this you can reframe the way you view uncertainty, and you can learn this from practicing artists. Rather than fear the unknown, they explore it. Rather than try to control the mystery, they let it guide, teach, and share new information. Artists know that deep within the mystery and unknown is not more chaos, but wisdom, intelligence, and beauty.

the art & practice of trust

CHAPTER TWO

Remembering ~ Forgetting

British child psychologist, D. W. Winnicott, first coined the terms True Self and False Self to recognize the parts of ourselves that are authentic and true and the parts that are not.

The belief is that when we're born we are fully our True Self. At birth we're open, receptive, and fresh from the Source of Life. Not yet shaped by expectations, a small child is free to express his or her true nature and others are free to fully offer love and acceptance. As babies, it is not very long before we begin to adapt to please others or to survive in our environment. We learn how to shape our behavior in order to fit in and remain connected to our caregivers. In doing this we develop a False or Adapted Self and may align less to our inner truth, our True Self.

As we grow we may begin to identify first and foremost with our Adapted Self and often find it hard to listen and connect to our deeper truth. Yet it is always there, always present, and always available to us if we are willing to listen.

What does our True Self look like?

I often ask people to tell me what they feel like when they are at their best. How about you? Take a moment and write down some words that describe how you feel when you are at your best and life is flowing.

Here are a few adjectives that often come up and that describe our True Self.

~True Self~

- Open and expansive
- Sees in terms of possibilities
- Connected to something greater than yourself
- Present. Lives in the moment.
- Sense of ease and flow. Synchronicity and chance happenings.
- Positive and inspiring
- Courageous
- Trusts
- Lighthearted and playful.
- Generous
- Sense of belonging
- Cares about helping others and the greatest good
- Source of true power.
- Lives in the heart. Loves.

This is the place, found within each of us, where we access our connection to our true Source of Power. True power comes from knowing and trusting the wisdom that comes from within.

When I write about discovering and trusting your inner wisdom, I am referring to trusting something much greater than the limited way in which we may perceive ourselves.

This path honors the intelligence that is at the Source of Life and sets the intention to align with it, listen to it, and be guided by it.

What does our Adapted Self look like? How do we know when our actions or behaviors are coming from this place instead of our True Self?

When we are in the Adapted Self, our sense of worth is coming from the outside in. How others perceive us defines, in our perception, who we are and our self-worth. It is a place of false power because the power comes from things that can all be lost or taken away and from what others think about us rather than what we know about ourselves.

Think of a time when you felt stressed, confused, or overwhelmed. Take a moment to write a few words to describe how that felt.

Here are some of the words that describe Adapted Self.

~ Adapted Self ~

- Lives in the head and rationalizes.
- Sees in terms of limitations
- Never enough. Needy and restless
- Tends to focus on the weaknesses of self and others
- Worried, fearful or intense
- Strives to be different, stand out
- Needs to be in control. Distrusts.
- Tight, constricted
- Sees self as separate and apart from others
- Must prove worth through doing
- Strives to compete and win at all costs
- Focused on self
- Lives in the past or worries about the future
- A false sense of power

Both of these 'selves' are within us all, and most of us move back and forth between the two on a daily basis. But take a moment and think about this. What would it be like to live more fully from your True Self? If you could increase, by just 10%, the amount of time you spend in your True Self, how would that change your life?

When faced with job loss, illness, aging, financial worries. or divorce, it's easy to get stuck or feel completely lost and disconnected from your True Self and, therefore, your own wisdom. You may feel alone, overwhelmed, anxious, worried, frustrated, or any other number of feelings and emotions that create tightness in our minds, hearts, and bodies. In this constricted space we are often unable to hear, sense, or feel what is possible, and fear can overwhelm us.

What would it be like if you knew that regardless of what

you were facing, you could find your way back to your own wisdom and take action from that place of freedom and confidence? How then would you live?

In the next chapter you will learn more about The Way of Discovery Pathway. It will help guide you through transition and change and increase your Self-awareness and Self- trust.

The Way of Discovery Pathway

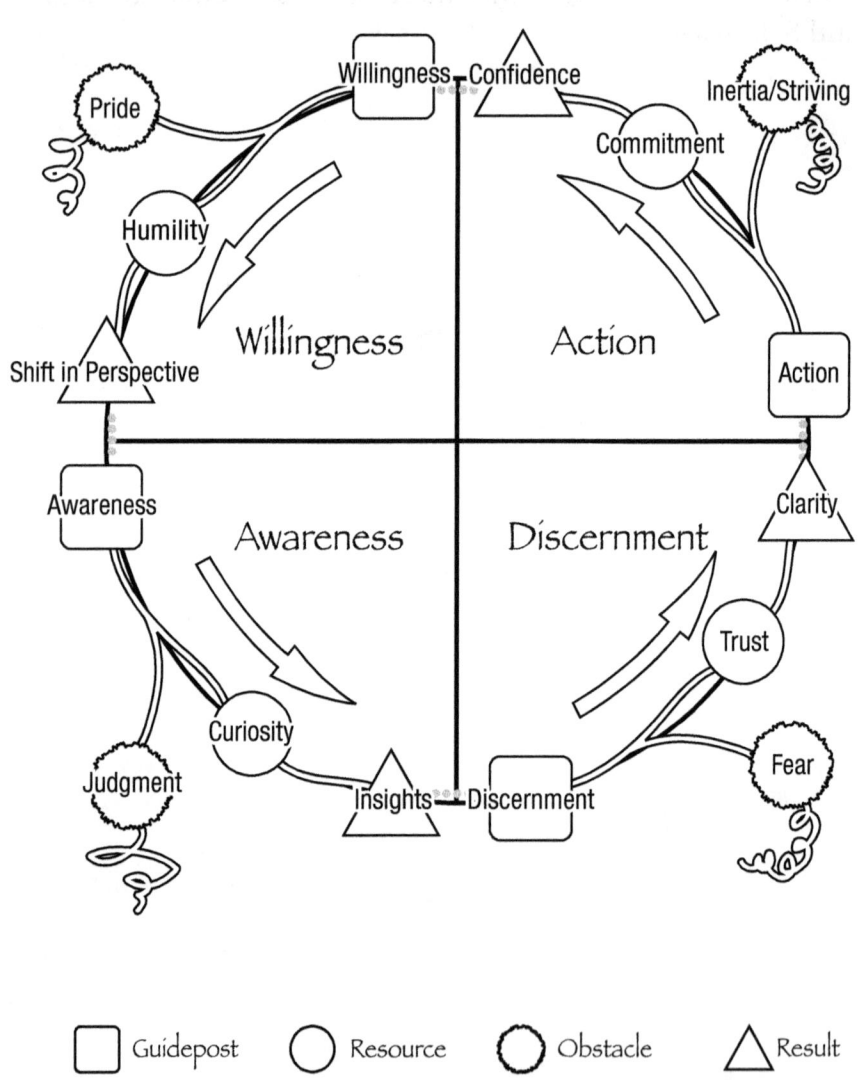

CHAPTER THREE

The Way of Discovery

The Way of Discovery is a pathway to help create, build and sustain trust.

There are four quadrants—willingness, awareness, discernment, and action—with four guideposts of the same names that lead you forward.

The first **guidepost** is **willingness**. It is through your willingness to open up to what is possible that you enter into the pathway. As you may have built well-protected walls around your beliefs or perceptions, the **resource** of **humility**, a modest and unassuming approach, is needed in order to pass this guidepost. The **obstacle** is **pride**, any pattern that takes you into self-inflation or separateness from life and others. The **result** is a **shift in perspective**, a broadening of understanding that offers hope.

Awareness, the second **guidepost**, is an opportunity to gather information and gain new perceptions. It requires the **resource** of **curiosity**, choosing to pay attention to what is happening (or has happened) with fresh eyes, ears, and all your other senses. The **obstacle** is judgment. The **result** is **insights** and new information.

The third guidepost is **discernment**. Discernment requires that you choose the **resource** of **trust** and rely on your own wisdom – found in your heart, mind, and body – to make a decision. The **obstacle** is **fear,** and the **result** is **clarity**. It is from clarity that we move into action.

Action, the fourth **guidepost**, requires the **resource** of **commitment**. The **obstacle** is **inertia** and/or **over striving**. The **result** is increased **confidence**, a sense of ease and freedom, and a sense of flow. You build inner confidence each time you choose to trust your True Self and act on your own wisdom.

The pathway is by its very nature dynamic and not time sensitive. Sometimes you will go through a significant transformative time and the quadrants may seem to take forever. Other times, the whole process and flow will happen in a flash.

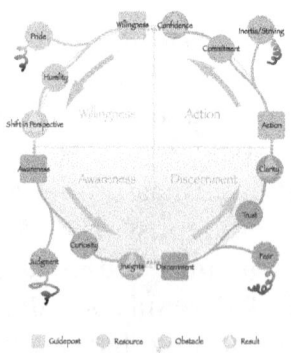

The guidepost, resources, obstacles, and results are represented by symbols.

The squares represent the four guideposts.

The clean circles represent the resources.

The jagged-edged circles with the tail represent the obstacles.

And the circle with a triangle inside represents the results.

The first part of this book, Chapters 4-8, explains the different parts of the path. Chapter 9 will help you pull it all together and offer practices to develop more skillfulness as you navigate.

There are 4 choices we repeatedly face between the resource and the obstacle within each quadrant. Choosing the resource will bring you freedom. The obstacle will always bring you into a tightened and constricted place,

We enter the pathway through willingness. The task of this quadrant is to open your mind and allow a shift in perspective so you can see things differently. It is this quadrant that is the foundation upon which all the other quadrants build.

I invite you now into the way of discovery....

The Way of Discovery Pathway

The Quadrant of Willingness

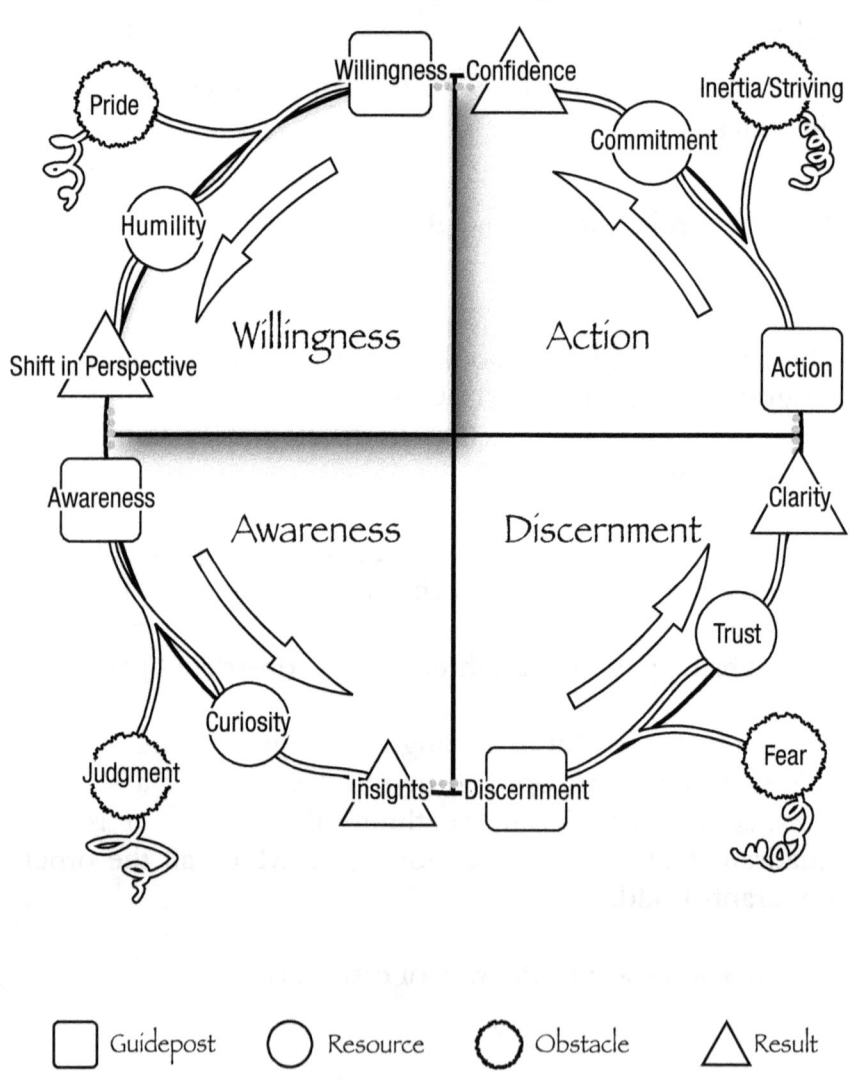

CHAPTER FOUR

Willingness

Are you willing?

"The greatest war in life within each individual is between the intellect and the heart where the heart is saying 'this is so' and the intellect is saying 'I don't understand, therefore I don't believe'."

Author unknown

It all begins with willingness, a willingness to let go of what we think we know and open our mind to what is possible. It sounds like such a simple concept—this idea of letting go, but it can be quite challenging and most difficult because it requires both courage and humility. Courage is needed to be vulnerable, and humility is required to see things with an open heart and an open mind.

By its very nature, willingness requires a leap of faith. When you are willing to make the choice to let go of your assumptions, even if it is just for a moment, you open yourself up to being influenced and having your perceptions changed. You may feel vulnerable, and many of us don't like that feeling. So this guidepost, right at the start, invites you out of your comfort zone and asks you to be willing to let your guard down.

Take a moment and read through this short list of questions. Read them out loud, and as you answer yes or no, notice the ones in which you sense a closing down in your mind and the ones in which your mind stays open. No need to justify or analyze. This is simply an exercise in noting willingness.

~ Are you willing... ~

- To go to a party alone?
- To try something you may not be good at?
- To tell the truth?
- To ask for help?
- To make a lot of money?
- To have courageous conversations?
- To admit you were wrong?
- To help another in need?
- To not have the answer?
- To follow another's lead?
- To be authentic and real?
- To be silly?
- To take a stand alone?
- To excel and be seen by many?
- To speak freely in front of others?
- To be in silence?
- To forgive?
- To be happy?

Hopefully, you found some "no's" in the list, and you were able to feel what it is like when your mind closed down. Many times it doesn't matter if we choose to close down, but when we are finding our way through uncertainty and want to connect most deeply with our 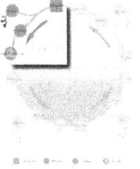 own wisdom, opening our minds up to what is possible is important. Doing this allows you to see things in new ways and be flexible in your thinking.

I went to visit Tim (short for Thelma) Edwards, a friend of my mother's. Tim was a very successful commercial realtor in the 1960s, a time when few women were in the workforce. My mom had been a traditional homemaker devoted to raising four children, nurturing a long-term marriage and keeping a home. Had they met earlier, both would have been too involved in their own worlds and too apart to let the other in. However, they met when in their late 70s and saw in each other unfulfilled parts of themselves. Rather than feeling jealous or put off, they formed a deep bond.

Over a light breakfast, I listened to stories of Tim's life, of deals made and risks taken. Her blue eyes were penetrating and seemed ageless as she related her adventures. She loved business and all the intricacies of it and still, at 88, was passionate about new opportunities. As I listened to her, I found myself wondering what she knew that gave her the confidence to take such bold steps. "Now that you have lived this long, as you look back, what do you think were the three most important things you've learned in life?" I asked.

Without hesitation, she said, "The first is to set goals. Without them, how do you know that you've gone where you wanted to go?" She followed with, "The second is love, specifically to know how to give and receive it. In fact, I think now that this is the most important thing of all." She hesitated for a moment, then looked me in the eyes. "The third is to open your mind to possibilities. There are too many people who limit themselves just because they won't open up their minds."

I slumped back in my chair and let her words sink in. I hadn't thought that my mind was closed, but when she said that, for a moment, I went blank. I realized my mind had been closed! I had not been able to imagine how I would be successful as an entrepreneur. I had a dream that I wanted to make real, but now that I was in the midst of trying to make it work, I didn't see *how* it could happen. I needed to open my mind and start feeding what was possible rather than feeding my fears, doubts, and worries. Although I was scared, what she said made sense and I decided to take action. When I went home, I met with someone who helped me create a new business plan, and I became more active in my community. I started extending myself more, and low and behold, business began to grow.

The practice of willingness is about opening up and creating space – in the mind, heart, and body. When you're stuck, afraid, worried or angry, creating space seems counterintuitive. Our basic human nature tugs on us to do the opposite -- to focus, tighten up, avoid, deny, or run away. We may constrict and draw in, which only limits our ability to be creative or effectively problem solve. That's okay when you are in a life- threatening crisis because that type of thinking will save your life. But when facing a transition or in times of uncertainty, openness and flexibility are needed, and a closed way of thinking will limit you and keep you from finding a sense of direction and flow.

Willingness

Closing down is a habit, which, like all habits, becomes unconscious. We do it routinely, without thinking, especially in the midst of change. There is much written about our ability to make a choice, but it is worth a quick review.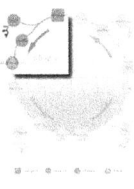

You may assume that when there is a stimulus some sort of response is automatic. For example, if someone is rude, I have to be rude in return. Or, if I'm offered a job, I must accept. Or, if there is a letter in my mailbox from the IRS, I have to be immediately anxious.

This way of thinking is represented in the diagram below.

Stimulus → Response

Yet, we may forget that between every stimulus and response is a space.

Stimulus →   → Response

In this space we can choose our response.

Stimulus → Choice → Response

This is where your true freedom lies, in your ability to

choose. You can decide what to do rather than feel that you have react to what happens to you.

This pathway will make visible choices that will empower you and also make visible those choices that will not. All of the resources will empower you and keep you connected to your Self. All of the obstacles will pull you away, distract you, and tie up your energy.

It may be hard to open up your mind, especially in the midst of difficulty, stress, or change. It is often seen as giving something up rather than opening up to something new. You may feel vulnerable. In that case I invite you to do a practice.

Here are three practices that will help open the heart and relax the body which, in turn, will help you widen your perspective so that you can see your situation in a new way.

The practice of gratitude

It doesn't matter who you are, life is going to challenge you and there will be difficulties. As Wallace Stevens says, "It's not everyday that the world arranges itself into a poem." In the meantime, things happen that we don't like, don't want, or don't think we can handle. However, remembering what we are grateful for opens up our hearts and minds and often makes whatever we're struggling with seem more manageable. Take a few minutes to write out ten things you are grateful for and notice how you feel afterwards.

The practice of generosity

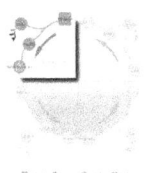

Often the times we feel the least generous are the times we need to be the most generous.
Have you noticed when you give to others who are in need how good it feels? I discovered when feeling sorry for myself, doing something for someone else shifts my whole perception. The emotions of fear, sadness, frustration, or worry take us *into* ourselves, and we become preoccupied with self. Giving and thinking about others brings us *out* of that self-focused thinking. What could you do right now to help to another?

The practice of breathing

Try this: Begin to pay attention to your breath. Without changing it, notice how you are breathing. Close your eyes and feel your breath as it comes in and out of your body. When you are ready, move your right hand to your chest and place your left hand on your belly. Continue breathing and notice which hand rises when you inhale. Is it your right hand? If so, you're not alone. The right hand lifting up indicates chest breathing, which signals to the body's intricate feedback system that danger may be present and that there is a reason to be stressed. When we consistently breathe this way, the body can remain on alert and tight. Want to learn a simple way to relax and quiet your body? Simply move your right hand down to your left, so that both hands rest on your belly. As you inhale, feel the rise of your belly; as you exhale, feel the release. Take five deep full breaths and notice how you feel.

Willingness can be challenging. If you are attached to the way you are perceiving a situation it is easy to mistake your truth for <u>the</u> truth. It is difficult then to open up and see things differently.

Fortunately, we have the resource of humility, and when we make the choice to approach life with humility, many more opportunities become visible.

● Resource: Humility

The root word of <u>humility</u> comes from the Indo-European word, "ghom," best translated as "humus." It means the dark, organic material in the soil that is produced by the breakdown of vegetable or animal matter. It is often called compost, a product rich in minerals and ideal for gardening.

For us, humility allows the breakdown of our adapted self or ego and the emergence of our true Self. Humility helps us to let go of seeing our self as separate and apart and instead reminds us that we all belong to life and each other. Like compost, when added to our lives, it provides richness – in the form of truth and connection.

Humility represents the humus, the 'ground' of our being and keeps us in touch with our humanness. Each one of us is unique and yet part of a collective, a whole. We are different from—but not better than or worse than—others. It is the habitual tendency of the adapted self to set oneself apart, view others in overly competitive ways or try to be special. From this perspective life is often seen in terms of limitations and scarcity. You may feel that you have to fight with others to get your share of the pie and constantly compete to protect it. Humberto Maruarana, the great Chilean biologist and philosopher, says, "We do not see the world around us. We see the world we are prepared to see." With a limited perspective on life, it is easy to see only limitations and scarcity. This is life seen through the eyes of the adapted self.

I am not suggesting that to live a better life we must let go of our adapted self and that only through living our true Self are we real and authentic. Instead I am offering that both our adapted and true selves are needed in order to live a happy, productive life. It's the balance and the source of leadership that are often misaligned. When our leadership comes from our true Self then there is a natural balance that occurs between the two that allows for a healthy sense of self esteem, self respect and self acceptance. During times of uncertainty, it's more important than ever that our leadership come from true Self because it is from this place that we have the ability to tap into our greatest potential for problem solving, creativity and growth. It is through the resource of humility we begin to reestablish a healthy balance.

The limited view of the adapted self is challenged through the practice of humility. Instead of separateness, connection is valued. Instead of scarcity, abundance is acknowledged. Humility encourages approaching situations and people with reverence out of appreciation for the diversity and complexity of life. Therefore, we can let go of having to have the answers, being needy or insecure and instead show up to life in a respectful way that recognizes wholeness and diversity. Then we can discover endless possibilities and unbounded opportunities because we have tapped into one of the great principles that govern the universe, interdependence. Humility reconnects us with the full capacity for the basic kinship of being human and reminds us that we belong to something much bigger than the limited perception we may have of our self.

To be humble is to show up with a modest approach. It is not groveling, being weak, or meekly submitting, but rather it is an unassuming and respectful way of being. It requires courage and true power. We put aside our own assumptions and listen from an open place. When bestselling author and psychotherapist, Wayne Muller, was acknowledged for his success in working with others, he said, "My work is simply to be good company, to allow others to lean for a while on my unshakable belief in their inner fire. Even on the good days I cannot do more than this." He knows that it is not about him doing something for another; it is simply a matter of seeing the people before him for who they are until they can remember and connect again with their truth.

In the ancient practice of yoga, a forward bend is a posture of humility. For thousands of years people have been aware of the seductive side of our adapted self. Teachers and wise men addressed the issue 'head on' through the physical body .Try this the next time you are feeling out of sorts or having difficulty seeing something from another's perspective. Standing upright, allow your head to bow down, arms to drop and your hands to reach toward your feet. Your head is lowered below your heart. This is symbolic of subjugating the thinking mind to the wisdom within the heart (your true Self). Releasing what you think you know so that you can be open to new ways of seeing is encouraged by the action of physically releasing your head downward. Stay in the forward bend for a few minutes and then when you straighten up, take a few deep breaths,

maybe a short walk and reexamine your challenge. See if you notice a shift in the way you were thinking. In prayers or sacred rituals, bowing the head honors the recognition of wisdom beyond that of our ego, found instead in the depth and stillness of our heart.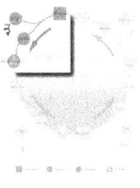
The intention to connect with our wisdom along with a physical action will often create all the opening you need to see something in a new way.

Out of all the resources along the pathway this is the one I personally work with the most because it is the one I so easily forget. Yet when I can remember to practice humility I discover life is full of unexpected support and unexplained happenings along with great love, acceptance and wisdom. It is from choosing to practice humility that we can experience what is possible.

As I completed the book, I was reflecting on the design for the cover and 'saw' the title along with a visual image of a feather floating downward. I was surprised and wondered why a feather? Over the next two weeks, it seemed everywhere I went I saw feathers on the ground. One morning while taking a walk, I was discouraged and felt as though I had a heavy weight on my shoulders. I was reflecting on some family issues that didn't seem to have an easy answer. Something caught my eye. I stopped and watched a small, ordinary brown feather, carried lightly by the wind, float down in front of me, gently landing on the grass nearby. It was peaceful and lovely to watch how tenderly the feather was supported and carried by the soft breeze. I thought about how soft yet resilient feathers are; how they are each unique and shaped in a way that allows a bird to take flight. I remembered a poem by Emily Dickenson called, 'Hope', sometimes referred to as 'Hope is the thing with feathers'. In her poem she uses the image of a bird to describe the abstract idea of hope and invites us to think of the feathers as enabling us to fly to a new beginning. The cover flashed into my mind. I realized that trust, like hope, also creates the space for new beginnings and that the feather is a visible symbol for the invisible support that comes with the willingness to trust.

If you find it difficult to practice humility, it may be the obstacle of pride that is pulling you away from expansiveness. As with all obstacles, pride can be seductive and often feels like the right choice, but rather than creating openness and expansiveness, the obstacle of pride will always lead you apart from others and your true Self.

 Obstacle: Pride

Pride is active any time we get caught in the behaviors that set us above or apart from others. Anything that creates self-importance, self-inflation or excessive self-reliance is part of the pattern of pride.

When you have done something well or feel good about an accomplishment, that's healthy pride. It's important. It reinforces feelings of capability and competence and builds self-esteem and self-worth. It feels good to have pride in work, relationships, and appearance. My client Sue tells me, "When I have tended to my flower-boxes and the grass is cut and my windows are clean, I feel proud as I look at my home. The work and attention has paid off, and I feel good."

Healthy pride is clearly visible in the Olympics. As the winner's national anthem is played and their country's flag is raised, tears often come to the eyes of those on the podium. The sense of pride in the accomplishment is palpable, even to those looking from afar.

But what about the other side? What about unhealthy pride? What price is paid when we exhibit patterns of self-inflation or are unwilling to admit that we are wrong? What happens when we think we are right – when we are so certain – that we have closed our mind to other possibilities?

There are all sorts of little ways that pride can creep in. It manifests in one-upmanship, always having to be the one in the know, trying to impress others, never admitting wrongdoing and not being willing to ask for help.

Whereas humility says '"I don't know," pride says "I absolutely know." Whereas humility opens the door to opinions, unhealthy pride closes it because pride has no need to know what others think. It already knows. Pride makes assumptions and then stands by them regardless of what other information comes in. Pride is invested in being right because self-worth may be at stake. Thoreau said it well: "How can we remember our ignorance, which our growth requires, when we are using our knowledge all the time?" Making assumptions and then standing by them at all costs is one of the ways pride affects our thinking and our ability to shift our perspectives. Most importantly, unhealthy pride constricts and keeps us from listening to our truth.

A client and I had been talking about pride and how easy it is to think we know. In one of our sessions, she told me this story. "Recently an issue came up with my sister," she said. "It was one we have dealt with for so long. Growing up there was a lot of competition between us. I tend to be pushy and she is stubborn and both of us like to be right. I can tell on the phone when I have gone too far with my suggestions. It suddenly feels like there is a dark, heavy presence on the line. Usually, I think I know what is happening and begin to analyze what I think it is, telling her what she's feeling and why. I used to think I was right and hated that I might be wrong. However, my way has never brought much success. In fact, we'd often end the calls quickly, both feeling a bit ruffled. But lately I've simply been asking if I've offended her. The first time she was so taken back. She said, 'No,' very quickly. But I just wait now, and eventually she tells me what has annoyed her or caused her to withdraw. I'm usually surprised. Rarely is it what I thought it was. This is not easy for me as I don't like being wrong, and I like to tell people what I think, but it's worth it. Our relationship is stronger than ever and we don't end our calls irritated any more."

Besides thinking we have all the answers, another way pride shows up is in the unwillingness to ask for help.

Laura told me a story of her daughter who had offered to clean up the kitchen. At five years old that was a big task, and it wasn't long before she was a bit overwhelmed. When Laura came into the kitchen to check on her, she found her sitting on the floor with a broken plate and food scattered all around. She looked up at her mom with trusting eyes and said, "Mom, could I have a little help here, please?" We laughed when she told me that story and commented on how hard it gets as we get older to ask for help when we need it. For some reason I believed for years that I had to figure things out myself and that the burden of finding my way was on my shoulders alone. I didn't like being vulnerable, but I didn't realize that I was denying myself joy and a feeling of being connected and supported by others.

Asking for help is natural and makes sense. How willing are you to ask for help? On this pathway of self-discovery and self-trust, as I 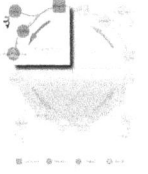 began to learn and experience more personal growth and awareness, I reached out for help and was fortunate to be on the receiving end of gifted healers, guides, therapists, and teachers. I had always valued fierce independence over interdependence, so to reach out when I was feeling vulnerable was hard, yet one of the smartest things I have done. I came to understand that I don't need to do everything on my own and that asking for help is not a weakness but a sign of inner strength.

Choosing pride over humility limits our ability to see opportunities in the midst of challenges. As you may notice on the model, pride leads us only downward. There is no way to a new perception when we are fixed on believing we are right or trying to compete or be better than others.

If you find yourself caught in pride and you're finding it difficult to open your mind to other possibilities, take some psychological space. Pause, give yourself some time, stop interacting with anyone, and step aside from whatever you are doing. Choose to open up to the possibility that there is another way to look at a situation and be willing to discover it. Take deep breaths, a walk, hum a favorite song. These simple activities will help you pause long enough to see things in a new way. The shift can be quite subtle. Sometimes all we need is one opening, one new thought, or one new possibility to surface and we are closer to a new perspective and one step closer to reconnecting with our own wisdom.

The shift out of pride and into willingness and humility will allow you to move toward the desired result—a shift in perspective.

 Result: A Shift in Perspective

The weather was 75 degrees with a slight breeze, so I threw open the windows and doors and turned up my music. The sweet smell of blooming jasmine floated in – along with a large black carpenter bee. I watched as the bee explored the kitchen space. Large, even for bees, they look intimidating, but they rarely sting people. They prefer to eat wood. The bee decided to return to the back yard and headed toward the window, but instead of going outside, he bounced up against the closed glass. Frustrated, over and over, he hit the window, buzzing loudly and clearly annoyed.

I cranked open the side panel of the window and used a piece of cardboard to guide him toward the opening. He wanted nothing to do with this and instead intensified his furious banging against the glass. I tried a number of times to gently direct him toward the opening and could only get him so far before he would jump above or around the cardboard and zip back to his corner. He was focused on what he wanted and what he wanted was to go through that glass. He could see the outside, so why should he move somewhere else? After four tries, I successfully got him to the open window where he flew off without hesitation.

As I watched him go, I couldn't help thinking how often I am like that bee. I can get so focused on what I want that I don't pay attention to help being offered that will move me toward my open window. Watching the bee, I felt my perspective shift. When something happens that is not part of a plan, it is so easy to get mad, frustrated, or defensive. But what about thinking that when something unexpected or challenging occurs, maybe life is moving us to a more advantageous place and we just don't know it? What if life, regardless of the outside situations, is trying to help us out? I can think of times, when just like the black bee, I could see what I wanted and was convinced that if I just worked harder I would get it, and yet it remained elusive. I have knocked over and over on a door that was never going to open. Then something happened that pushed me in another direction, and although I may have been furious or in great fear at the time, in looking back I can see that what was gained was truly beneficial.

You may feel that you have gotten where you are in life precisely because of sheer will and your own determination. You dug down deep and made something happen and maybe even for years it has worked well. But now, you may be facing something that is challenging you in new ways, and increasing your efforts of hard work and determination is not enough. It may be a job loss, an illness, a divorce, or any change that pulls you into a place of uncertainty and unknown. It can be unsettling, and the normal reaction is to tighten up or to intensify efforts. It can feel as if you are in a small, dark room with no light. You want to get out, but you don't even know where to begin. This guidepost, of willingness, invites you instead to let go of having to do it all yourself and open up to being in a more conscious relationship with your true Self: that part of you that is wise, all knowing and endlessly resourceful.

When you are willing to look at things in a new way, you will experience a shift in your perception. It's as though someone opens a door and a shaft of light appears in an otherwise dark room. It's an opening, subtle or slight, but still there. All of sudden, something has changed, and you are seeing or sensing something in a new way.

This is the result you are looking for with this guidepost. When you sense that, you are ready to move on.

Willingness and humility are the foundations of this pathway. Try asking yourself these questions the next time you find yourself caught in a struggle.

What am I assuming to be true? What can I let go of to create space? What is the pay off in choosing pride over humility? Is there another way to look at this?

For practices and exercises that will strengthen your understanding of this quadrant, look at Chapter Nine under the heading Willingness.

Willingness

The Way of Discovery Pathway

The Quadrant of Awareness

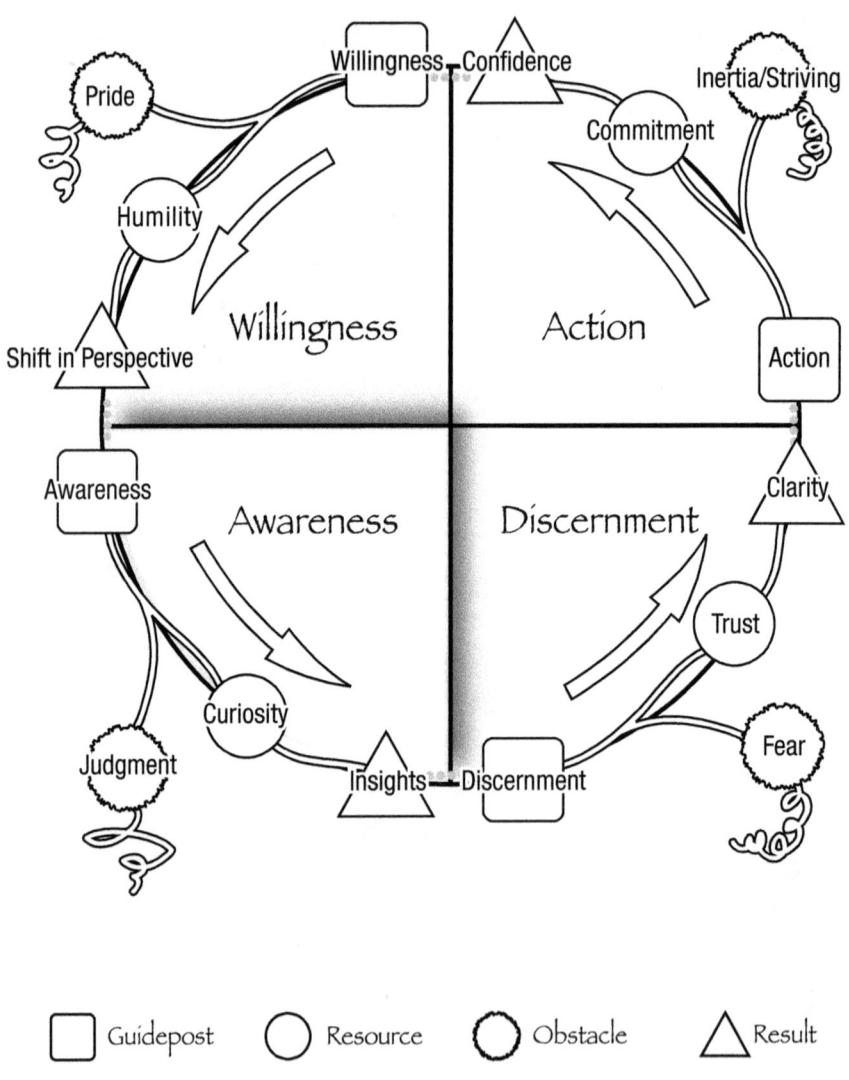

CHAPTER FIVE

Awareness

Will you pay attention?

"We are disturbed not by what happens to us, but by our thoughts about what happens." Epictetus

The second guidepost is Awareness. With Awareness it is as if you walk toward the shaft of light, open the door, and see in front of you a large open field waiting to be explored.

Whereas, the first quadrant of Willingness facilitates a

shift of mind that allows you to see something new, this quadrant, Awareness, is about staying open and gathering information long enough to be satisfied that you have all the input you need before making an informed decision.

Sometimes paying attention or being in awareness brings beauty, stillness, and pleasure, as in witnessing a sunrise or experiencing an intimate moment with another.

Other times it brings unwelcome surprises and strong emotions such as fear, anger, or anxiety. In true awareness you don't know what will surface and become visible. That is not only part of what makes it so interesting, but also what makes it so challenging. The task is to simply pay attention, gather information, and stay open.

One way to do this is to become present to the moment. It is so easy to get caught up in the busyness and activity of life. Hectic schedules, work commitments, and family obligations can fill your day and pull you away from quiet time with yourself. The fact is that the more life speeds up, the more we can lose touch with the silence and quiet in the present moment. For the purposes of this guidepost, knowing how to still the mind and be present in the moment helps you hear the different voices that make up your inner conversations and, more importantly, sense your own wisdom. Listen to your thoughts. Your thoughts drive your actions, so listen to your thoughts for the truth or untruths they bring.

Simply stated, we are not our thoughts. Thoughts come into our minds and leave like clouds moving in the sky. They appear and disappear. It's our attachment to our thoughts that causes us problems, especially the thoughts that we believe can cause great joy or suffering.

To discover what is true, you can question your thoughts and listen from that deeper part of yourself to discern their validity. Byron Katie, author of, *Loving What Is*, teaches that it is the job of the mind to validate and hold in place what it believes. But when you question 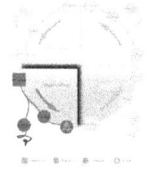 the truth of something that you may have taken for granted, it frees the mind up. Without the job of holding something in place, your mind can open up to other options. Simply ask yourself, "Is it true?" the next time you hear a thought that encourages you to judge or close down, and notice what happens.

Also, pay attention to the words you use and you will discover much about what you are thinking.

Julie had been in corporate America for twenty years. After much thought she decided to leave her job and start her own business as a business coach. She would tell her friends, "Yes, it's true. I'm leaving and going out on my own as a consultant. I'm getting ready to jump off the cliff." One time as she routinely said this, one of her coaching colleagues asked her how she felt when she said she was going to jump off a cliff. "A bit nervous" was her reply. "What about saying, 'I'm getting ready to leap, and a net will be there for me'?" suggested one friend. That sounded better she said, but it was when another friend suggested, "How about 'I'm getting ready to leap and soar'?"..... that Judy said she felt the shift. There was a freedom she discovered with that suggestion that created space in her mind and opened up her heart. Suddenly, rather than jump and go down the side of a cliff, she was going to soar!

So often we don't pay attention to the words we speak and miss opportunities to make visible our inner conversation.

Notice the words you use to describe yourself, your situation, or others. Are they empowering, positive, and do they lead you forward? If not, take some time to reflect and choose words that do.

Curiosity, the resource for the quadrant of Awareness, is your greatest ally. The more curious you are, the more insights you will receive.

To read more about how to be in the silence and practice presence, look in Chapter 9, under Awareness. There you will find exercises that will help you develop a greater understanding of this practice.

 Resource: Curiosity

Curiosity is a powerful ally. It is one of the most important and greatest resources for finding your way. When in transition or change, the right question at the right time has the ability to shake us up and redirect our thinking. Questions such as; what is needed right now? What has heart and meaning for me at this time? What is wanting to happen? or What do I really want? all help shift attention from worry, concern and fear to reflection and productive thinking. Curiosity has a wondering, musing, childlike quality that encourages exploration. All of the great inventors and explorers began by being curious about some thing, place, or idea. Their inquisitiveness drew them forward.

We were naturally curious as children. We all went through a stage of asking questions like, "Why do trees grow? What makes the color red? Why are you so tall? and "How do butterflies fly?"

What caused some of us to stop being so curious? Was it that sometimes our inquisitiveness got us into trouble? Did we hear just once too often the old adage that curiosity killed the cat? Or do we connect curiosity somehow with meddling or prying, and therefore deem it unseemly?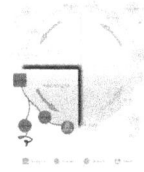

Curiosity directs your attention, and what you put your attention on grows, whether it is a houseplant, a relationship, or a dream. On this pathway, curiosity is a powerful ally that helps you stay open while you receive information so that you will have a greater picture of the challenge you face. Being curious will keep you from falling into the trap of judgment, which closes the door on learning something new.

One day, riding in an airport shuttle, I overheard part of a conversation. Two friends had been going back and forth for a while and finally one said, "I don't know what to do." Her friend responded by saying, "Yes, you do, and when you are ready to hear it, you'll ask yourself, and you'll find out." This woman knew what the great sages know – that we can find the answers to our questions if we will simply ask, and then listen to our inner Self and its wisdom.

In great spiritual traditions, there is an emphasis on the deep questioning of life. This questioning allows a conversation to take place between yourself and a profound, compassionate wisdom that answers. When in a transition or place of uncertainty, this type of inquiry is very helpful. Erich Schiffmann, respected yoga teacher and author of *Yoga, The Spirit and Practice of Moving into the Stillness*, says that when it is clear that you don't know something, it makes sense to ask. He uses the example of driving in an unfamiliar town and becoming lost. He says you wouldn't hesitate to stop and either look at a map or ask someone for directions. He goes on to say, "It is the same here; however, instead of looking at an external map or asking someone else for directions, you ask inwardly, using your mind to commune with the Infinite Mind...You ask inwardly of your Self—like a wave to the ocean, a cell to the brain, or a cloud to the sky. You ask the larger part of you, the part that knows. You ask and listen and lo and behold...you find yourself knowing." Each one of has this ability. It just takes time and practice and a willingness to suspend disbelief. It also takes willingness to feel.

To ask this type of inner question and stay open and curious to information as it comes in, you have to feel your feelings. If you cannot feel what your body and heart are telling you, then you will miss insights and valuable information.

We are feeling beings. Feelings are a rich and fundamental part of the human experience. They bring us information about the state of our relationships with others, tell us where our personal boundaries have been crossed or invaded, and allow us to experience love and intimacy at the deepest levels. Being able to feel is one of your greatest gifts.

Your feelings can be rich, sensual, tender, exquisite and sacred- the spice of life. They can also be unpredictable, messy, unexpected, unwelcome, unsettling, and overwhelming. You may wonder if you can trust them, let alone survive them, especially when you get caught in fear, rage, or terror.

Feeling your emotions when you were younger may

not have been safe. You may have been humiliated, judged, laughed at, or abandoned when you expressed what you felt. You may have grown up pretending that you didn't feel what you felt or ignoring emotional promptings just to survive. If your feelings were too intense, not knowing how to process them, you may have blocked them out using foods, drugs, alcohol, sugar, or mindless activities to distract or comfort yourself.

~ Have you heard or been part of a conversation like this? ~

"How do you feel about that?"
"Well, I think . . ."
"No, no, how do you *feel*?"
"I told you, I'm thinking."

Feelings can be tricky, and it's not unusual for people who have lived their lives cerebrally to find it difficult to feel. Over thinking and not consciously feeling can become habitual.

Nancy, a coaching client, told me once that she felt like there was an overgrown pathway filled with weeds between her mind and heart. Each worked well on its own, but they didn't connect. She was either in her mind or in her heart but didn't know how to be in both. This is common. I shared with her that by having a clear pathway between her heart and mind she would have a full and more whole approach to gathering information. Plus, it was her birthright. We all have the ability to tap into the wisdom of our heart and mind.

She was intrigued by the possibility and wanted to learn more. What was interesting about Nancy was the courage it took for her to admit this. She was a minister, and yet she realized that she was over thinking everything. Her humility and willingness to open up was inspiring.

As the famous psychologist Carl Jung discovered with his personality testing, some of us are naturally thinkers and some are naturally feelers, but that does not preclude anyone from feeling emotions. Feelings, combined with our intellects, guide and direct us. In order for us to be really alive, we have to feel.

To connect with your feelings and your heart, take a moment and be still. Draw your attention to the center of your chest and visualize your heart. Feel the front as well as the back of your chest. Then think of a time when you were very happy or a time when you felt love. If that's difficult, then think of someone or something that you love. Let yourself sense it, feel it, and remember it as clearly as you can. As you breathe, inhale from the back side of your chest, between your shoulder blades. Then exhale through your solar plexus. Keep doing this for three or four minutes, and then notice how you feel. This type of connection with your heart has been found to reduce stress, as well as bring more joy and happiness into your life.

Use the resource of curiosity, to become more skillful and to stay engaged as you explore your inner world. Ask yourself questions and listen for the answers. Be patient. Answers come in many ways, including flashes of insights or a sense of knowing. But they also come in the unexpected ways through dreams, serendipitous happenings, chance encounters, and a variety of unexplained coincidences. Practice being open to all your feelings and staying open, regardless of how much you may want to discount them. Learning this path is a practice in developing the relationship with your true 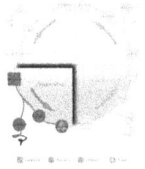 Self. What makes sense in the very realistic, day-to-day world is different from what makes sense in the world of inner exploration and Spirit. Give up trying to figure out how things happen and instead let yourself stretch out of your comfort zone and open up to discovery. For those of us who are skeptical, and I count myself in this group, this approach defies logic.

The symbol of the swan has always meant something special to me. I love their unique grace and beauty and when I was little ran to see them first when visiting the zoo. One time in the middle of a difficult decision, I followed my instincts and quickly made a choice. Immediately, as I hung up the phone, I felt a sense of concern. Did I make the right choice? Feeling unsettled, I asked for a sign to let me know if I had made the right choice at that time and then turned my attention elsewhere. A few hours later, getting into my car, I noticed a yellow truck that I had never seen before on my street. The driver walked up and handed me a card that said Swann Food Service. There on his truck was a large painted swan. I laughed and felt this amazing sense of playfulness. My worries left. I was reassured and found out later that yes, my choice did turn out to be a good one.

Remain open, be curious, and play with this resource. Listen with the intent to hear. It may be that your wisdom shows up in a physical prompting like a gut reaction. It may be that instead you hear a small, inner voice or maybe you see visions or get flashes of insights.

In a transition or a time that you are feeling lost, curiosity, aligned with your own wisdom, will move you forward and give you valuable information.

 Obstacle: Judgment

If you notice that instead of staying open, you find your mind closing down, you may have taken the turn into the obstacle of judgment.

Judgment, or being judgmental, is an obstacle which will lure you off the path and lead you down into a dead end. Judgement is the voice that tells you there is something wrong with you or another. It invites you to place blame, see things in terms of black and white, and disconnect from others.

There are many voices that speak to you in your head. We're so used to them that we often don't pay attention to them. Take a minute to sit quietly and listen to your inner dialogue. Sit in silence for about three minutes. You may hear... "What is this about? This is a waste of time. Come on... is it time to stop yet?"

This inner dialogue is running all the time. Some of the voices are more respectful and kinder than others. Some are downright cruel and disrespectful.

Think of the last time you did something embarrassing. Or the last time you were irritated with someone. Now listen to your inner dialogue. Write it out. Notice the judgments.

Judging ourself, others, or a situation creates a downward spiral that leads to comparisons, feelings of inadequacies, guilt, or resentment. Judgment of others creates distance, misunderstandings, finger pointing, and communication problems. You know  you are in judgment when you receive information and become defensive, feel justified, blame others, or jump to conclusions.

It is not uncommon that the more we are willing to stay open to information the more we hear that may unsettle us. There may be situations in our lives that show us to be selfish, unkind, or any number of unflattering states. Be a compassionate observer without harsh judgment or shame so you can connect with your true Self.

Our sense of flow and ease in life, is fueled by the relinquishing of judgment rather than by the refining of it.

But isn't judgment necessary when we need to figure something out or make decisions? Absolutely...but that comes later in the quadrant of Discernment. For this guidepost, Awareness, it's vital to stay curious and not judge. Later there will be a time that you will discern, but not now. This is the time to gather information so that you can see the bigger picture and stay connected with that wise, all-knowing part of yourself.

I was drawn to attend a silent retreat simply to see embodied what I had heard about for so many years – presence. Thich Nhat Hahn, a Vietnamese Buddhist monk, and fifty other monks and nuns were going to be in Santa Barbara for a weeklong mindfulness retreat. I had read some of Thich Nhat Hahn's books and found them to be simple, peaceful, and logical. I signed up to attend.

I heard there were going to be more than 1,300 people there. How would I feel living with so many strangers in close proximity for a week? What would I experience being in silence? How would it be to eat next to others and not talk? What would it be like to listen to this teacher?

I was not disappointed. His presence radiated peace and compassion, and I felt not only welcomed, but embraced. The mass of people, all doing their best to practice being in the moment, were like quiet, gentle animals, moving around respectfully. We greeted each other with nods at the silent meals and when we met on walkways. The first few days my mind was active and offered a running commentary about this or that. We were taught to let the thoughts come in and float by. So, as instructed, I practiced breathing, just noticing my thoughts and letting them go. I could feel my body relax and my mind start to quiet in a way I had never before experienced.

Unhurried, I ate meals in silence, chewing slowly, tasting each bite. The first few meals were challenging. But I found myself enjoying the slower pace, and my digestion was the best it had been in years.

At the retreat, there was a wide stretch of beach right below our dorm room. I decided to take a walk and kept my shoes on. Noticing darkened areas of sand that looked like oil, I purposely stepped over them in order to keep my shoes clean. Walking into my dorm room later, I noticed my roommate, sitting on the bed, scraping black-crusted oil off the bottom of her feet. Mentally taking note, I wondered why she wasn't more careful because the oil spots seemed so well marked in the sand.

The next day was beautiful and right after lunch I decided to go back to the beach and walk, but this time with my shoes off. Walking along, I again noticed the dark oil patches, and remembering my roommate, carefully stepped only on the whitest of sand. When I got to the 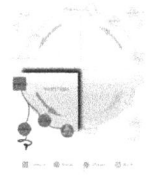 asphalt walkway leading back up to the campus, I saw a couple. The man was bent over at the waist, helping the woman clear the tar off the bottom of her feet. Again I wondered why people weren't more careful and felt a bit smug that I had watched out so carefully on my walk.

So sure was I of having clean feet that at first it didn't even register when I looked at the bottom of my feet and saw oil spots. How could this have been? I was so sure, so positive that I didn't step in any oil, and yet there it was all over my feet! My stomach and shoulders tightened up. I noticed I felt embarrassed and guilty. My stomach tightened as I judged myself.

During the week's practice we had learned how to step aside and witness thoughts rather than believe them. I visualized two versions of myself, one "me" walking right alongside the other "me," observing what was unfolding. Staying with my breath and listening to my thoughts, I suddenly realized how perfect I always tried to be and how I had judged others, in subtle ways, against my standards of perfection. Ouch. I also realized that when they fell short I felt better about me. Ouch again.

I kept breathing slowly and stayed open as feelings of embarrassment and voices of harsh judgment came up. Then suddenly I sensed a shift and a kind insight bubbled up to the surface of my mind. I heard, "Not perfection, compassion." Hearing this, the tightness left, and instead

I felt as if someone had wrapped comforting arms around me and offered kindness and understanding. I was able to relax and even smile to myself.

The great value of this practice of letting go of judgment comes when we can meet face to face with our humanness and offer ourselves forgiveness and compassion rather than judgment and shame. For many of us, so much energy is put into having to have it all together. It's exhausting, and it keeps us from feeling connected or having a sense of belonging with others. And, more importantly, it keeps us from our own wisdom, our own true Self. Freedom comes when we can let go and instead just be who we are: people doing the best we can in the situations of our lives.

Result: Insight

The result of the quadrant, Awareness, is insights. You begin to see, sense, and hear things in a new way and gain valuable information about your situation. Rather than feel trapped in seeing only the challenges, you will begin to see more opportunities.

Sam had accepted a new job in a new city. He'd had a difficult start in his life with a series of early losses that often left him feeling unsure of himself and tentative. We had been working together for quite a while, focusing on helping him trust himself more and not second-guess every choice he made. He had worked hard at developing a sense of inner confidence and direction, and I had seen a lot of growth. Now, at 25, he was going out on his own. We had worked together for the last year preparing him for this transition, and he had confidence in his ability to manage this change, although we knew it was definitely taking him out of his comfort zone.

When it was time for him to leave, we said goodbye, and, as I wished him luck, I reminded him of our scheduled call a few weeks away. He waved me off and said he was feeling strong and on task; although he would be on the call, he didn't think he'd need it. When we spoke on the phone a few weeks after he left, he was spiraling.

"I'm struggling. I'm feeling depressed and down," he said. "All my fears and doubts about myself have come back, and I feel like I'm fighting them off with a stick. I'm afraid I'm not going to be successful. And I feel so out of place here. I can't imagine ever being close with anyone, and now I'm feeling like I'm going to end up alone. I'm embarrassed to admit this, but I'm so stuck that I can't think of anything positive and I'm getting more and more isolated. My mind feels like it's starting to eat itself." He asked me what I thought. I was quiet and thinking of a way I could help him see this in a different way.

Then the most interesting thing happened. He said, "I wonder what I would say to myself if I was ten years down the road and looking back."

"What would that be?" I asked.

Sam immediately began to rattle off roughly the following: *What's really important right now? Don't worry. This is all just wasted energy . . . let it be. Be willing to fail. It's okay. Don't get down on yourself. Be fluid and free yourself up.* With each comment, he settled down, and by the end of our call, he was wondering what he had gotten so worked up about.

Navigating through these new waters, Sam wanted to trust his own wisdom, but with all the change and uncertainty, he became afraid and instead put his attention on fear. Then he got caught in harsh self-judgment. Because he had practiced trusting himself he became curious and opened up to receiving insights that helped him move forward. I asked him later what prompted him to ask himself that question, and he said that after he expressed what he was feeling, it just popped into his mind. Sam had replaced old habitual tendencies to feel victimized with new habits that supported his well-being.

This guidepost, more than any of the others, requires a certain steadiness as staying open to new information can be stressful, especially during times of transition and rapid change.

It is not unusual to have a number of insights yet, there is a point where you will feel that you have all the information you need to move on. It is subtle but similar to being ready to do something active after you have been on a long vacation. You have had enough, and you are ready to go. Move into discernment when you feel you have all the information you need to make a decision.

The next chapter is on discernment. There is a natural swing back and forth between awareness and discernment as direction or answers received are tested for truth and validity. There also comes a point when a decision must be made and often without enough information. This is where we lean into the resource of trust and step out into the unknown.

To learn more about how to handle stress, see Chapter 9, under the heading of Awareness.

Awareness

The Way of Discovery Pathway

The Quadrant of Discernment

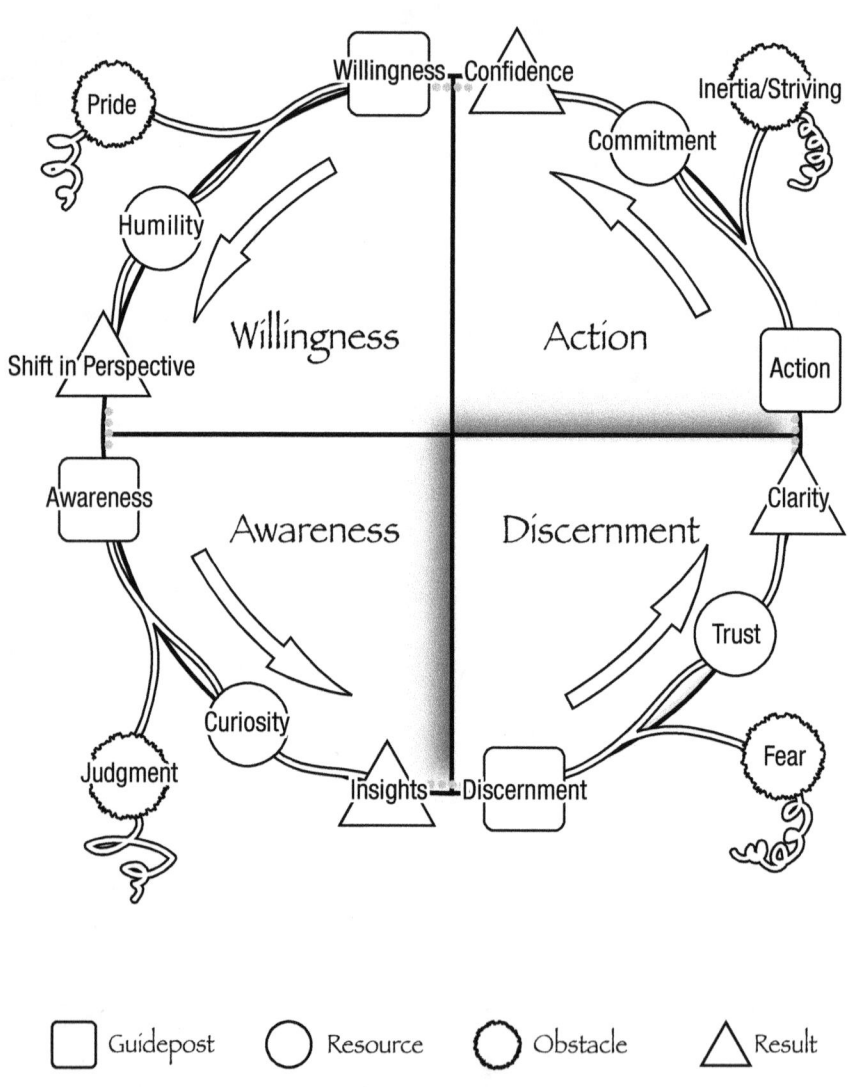

CHAPTER SIX

Discernment

Will you trust your Self?

*"Ultimately, we must learn to trust ourselves. When we do this intimately and intelligently, the world opens full of meaning before us.
We find that we ourselves are the doorway to a fathomless understanding of the source of life itself. We need only to learn to walk through it."*

James Thornton

Whereas willingness invites you in and awareness fills you up with insights, discernment is a narrowing-down process that takes the insights received and sorts through them to gain clarity. Discernment requires clear thinking, along with the willingness to pay attention to the tangible and intangible information of your mind, body and heart. Logical, practical decision making, along with paying attention to your intuition, serendipitous and synchronistic events, symbols, dreams, and chance happenings gives you a plethora of ways to listen and be guided by your own wisdom. This helps you draw on many different resources and aids you in making a wise choice, rather than limiting yourself to a few habitual tendencies.

When discerning, have a clear vision of what you desire and what you stand for. Also have a sense of your own purpose. Sometimes a big transition or period of unknown is giving you the opportunity to discover just that. If so, your vision would then be something similar to this: "My vision is the desire to know my purpose in life and live it." That is what you want to know. For other times of transitions or places of uncertainty, your vision may be simply to find your next step or to gain clarity around a new job, trip, or opportunity.

Your values reflect how you live your life and what is important to you. They help you know where to draw the line and what you will take a stand for. Values are represented by words such as integrity, achievement, generosity, or humor. In Chapter 9 there is information that you will find helpful on clarifying what you want and identifying your values, purpose and vision.

Developing the skills of discernment requires paying attention to the wisdom of the heart, mind, and body. If you have learned to rely mostly on your thinking for

Discernment

information, you may find that when your thinking gets muddled, you will need more time to gain clarity. Having access to the wisdom of the heart or the body can help.

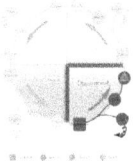

Sally, a lawyer for more than twenty years, writes everything down when making a decision. She creates a list of pros and cons and then decides on her plan of action. This worked well until she faced an emotional dilemma that didn't have a clear answer and involved hurting someone she loved. Stumped, she lived with the confusion and angst for nearly two years. When she was willing to listen and act on what her body was telling her, she found the right answer, and she was able to finally take action and end the relationship.

Mary, on the other hand, operates more from her feelings. She gets a light, expansive sensation in her heart when something is a yes and a closing in her chest when it's a no. This worked well until she came upon a situation that was very intense and she felt pulled in two different directions. She found herself eating too much, telling the same story over and over again, and looking to other people to tell her the way to go. It was when she sat down and logically worked through her options that she gained clarity and, like Sally, was able to act.

Strengths can become weaknesses when we depend on them too much. When it comes to making decisions, sometimes our strengths can be blind spots. I experienced this just recently. It was time to make a decision and I had all the information I needed, yet I wanted to get just a bit more. My strength is going deep into subjects, and I enjoy reflecting, exploring, and analyzing insights. In this case my strength worked against me. I began over analyzing and over thinking, and pretty soon I was caught in indecision. It was a good friend who said, "Enough already, make the decision, and get on with it." It was hard because I had "tied" myself up with all my thinking but I did make a decision and took action quickly. Later, I could see exactly what had happened, but at the time, my dependence on my thinking confused me. Decisions become easier to make when we learn how to access the resources found in the mind, body, and heart.

 Resource: Trust

The resource for the quadrant of Discernment is trust, specifically trusting that part of yourself, your true Self, which is wise, all-knowing, and interested in the greatest good.

According to cultural anthropologist and author Angeles Arrien in her book, *The Four-Fold Way*, "It takes courage to listen to and trust your true Self. Courage comes from the root word *coeur*, which is Norman French for heart. To have courage means having a heart that is *strong, full, open and clear*. Indigenous cultures believe that when you have these four qualities, it means that you have access to your whole heart and therefore you are able to stand in your truest sense of power and inner strength."

To trust your Self means that you have the courage to listen to your own wisdom, above all the other voices inside or out that praise, cajole, condemn, or distract and act on what is true for you.

This doesn't mean that you don't seek advice, feedback, ask for help, or encourage others' opinions because what they offer is often vital information. Instead, it means that you know that the final answer always lies within your own heart.

So many things conspire to pull us away from listening to our Self and our inner wisdom.
There is a constant barrage of messages that come our way and tell us that in order to be whole we need to buy, be, or do this particular thing. Through television and other media, the body and mind can become so over stimulated that we get used to a high level of intensity and find it's difficult to be present to life or ourselves. The foods we eat, the coffee and stimulants we ingest, the video games, even the music we listen to, can draw us further away. Just the thought of quieting down and sitting for a few minutes in silence can be overwhelming for some people. Yet, it's in the silence and the quiet that we connect with this part of our greater Self.

Listening is the key.

Think about when you are on the phone talking with someone who matters in your life. Think about how you listen for their response, how you want to hear what they have to say. When you ask a question, you listen, waiting for an answer. It's the same way here. You ask a question to that part of you within that holds unlimited wisdom and possibilities and is guiding you for your highest and best good. And you listen for an answer that will lead to clarity. Pay attention and notice what creates a readiness in your mind to receiving information. Are you listening with the intent to hear?

One client told me that for her this is like a quiet voice that bubbles up to the surface. If she is not careful, she'll miss it. Later, when she realizes it was a mistake not to have acted on it, she will remember that "bubble" moment.

Answers that lead to clarity come in many ways, including a process of formal logic, insights from others, a sense of knowing, a feeling, inner promptings, dreams, a song on the radio, serendipitous happenings, chance encounters, or unexplained coincidences. Answers on this pathway honor and recognize the tangible and the intangible ways that life speaks to us. There is a whole world of invisibles that are often ignored or judged as not valid simply because they are not seen with the eye and touched with the hand. And yet they are real and offer great wisdom.

Listening for an answer requested can be quick and direct or take a long time in coming. One of the biggest challenges is managing the edginess you may feel as you wait for the answer. It can almost feel like you are trying to sit still on top of a wild animal. You want resolution, you want answers now – but for whatever reason, it is not time. It can feel intolerable. Believe me, I sympathize and have been there many times. However, I have found that there is a type of readiness, similar to the ripening of fruit that occurs in a waiting period. If you move too quickly before the timing is right, you risk missing the full benefit found within a situation. This pathway is an art and like all art is a practice in trail and error. You learn as you go, and as you become more sensitive to your communication style with your Self, you will develop a greater sense of partnership and trust that helps relieve the impatience.

What if you're not sure you really want to hear an answer? Don't judge. Just be aware that for whatever reason, you're not quite ready, and need to go at it another way.

Discernment

* If you get stuck, rather than asking the same question again, try asking a question that helps you to see what might be in the way. For example, you could ask, "What is blocking me from getting clarity around this question?" or "What is it that I don't want to see?" 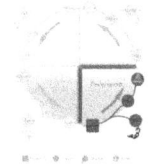 *If this becomes uncomfortable, take a break. Step away and give yourself time. It will come up at a later date. Sometimes things are too raw to be dealt with and need space.*

Have you ever had the experience of remembering an odd or unexpected story out of the blue? Out of nowhere something suddenly comes to mind. When that happens during a time that you are discerning, look for the link between what is happening in your life and the story itself. You might be surprised that there is relevance in it, and it may hold a key to helping you to see more clearly.

Psychiatrist Carl Jung taught that symbols are the language of the soul. Symbols bypass the logical mind and touch something deep within us that knows truth.

There are many books on this subject and wonderful people who are great resources in helping to interpret symbols, I encourage you to learn more, but remember that the final meaning of a symbol lies within you.

During a time of my life when I was feeling disconnected and a part from others, I remembered a story.

Growing up, I would hungrily wait for a television program in the 1960s filled with wild, imaginative stories that had terrifying twists at the end. One episode opened with a young, beautiful woman shopping at a department store. Feeling tired, she went into the bathroom and sat on a small sofa to rest. She fell asleep, and when she awoke, she discovered that the store had closed and she had been locked in. Annoyed at first, she tried all the obvious things—calling out for help, looking for an active phone or an alarm—but nothing worked, and so she finally gave up and decided that she would probably be there all night.

As she roamed around the store, she heard someone calling her name faintly: "Elizabeth…Elizabeth.…" At first, she was not sure she had heard anything, so she ignored the voice. But it became louder. She called out, "Who's there? Who's calling me?" But there was no answer. A bit unsettled, she continued to explore the dimly lit store. She heard it again—someone calling her name. It sounded like someone whispering loudly, "Elizabeth, Elizabeth.…" She was frightened, and again called out, "Who is there? What do you want?"

The rest of the show depicted her in unfolding stages of alarm as she moved around the store, wanting to get away but unable to leave and unable to find the source of the voice. Panicked, she decided to go up to another floor. She got into the elevator and pushed the button for the fourth floor. The elevator took her to the 13th floor—even though there were only 12 floors in the building.

The music built as she stopped at the 13th floor. Her eyes were wide with terror as the elevator doors opened to a storage room filled with mannequins, their shiny, plastic bodies standing in various poses. Trembling, she got out and tentatively walked forward into the space. She began to hear her name being called again, this time louder and louder—and not just one voice, but many. As she was just about to collapse with fear, one of the mannequins turned to her and said, "Well, it's about time, Elizabeth. You're long overdue. You were supposed to be back here six weeks ago."

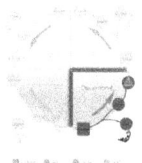

At that point, the other mannequins began to move and agree: "Yes, where have you been, Elizabeth?" There was a moment in which the terror and the confusion produced a stupor of thought. But slowly an understanding seeped in, and she remembered. She is a mannequin. It had been her turn to "be human" and live out in the world. Elizabeth had become so engrossed in life that she forgot to come back. She had forgotten who she was. In the next scene, the store is open the following morning and filled with busy shoppers. As the camera scans the room, we see Elizabeth, once again a mannequin standing with the others.

Visionary French philosopher Teilhard de Chardin was first to coin the expression, "We are not human beings having a spiritual experience. We are spiritual beings having a human experience." Rich, spiritual traditions remind us of this and liken this life to a forgetting process. Like Elizabeth in the story above, I had forgotten my truth and instead felt only the fear, resistance, and avoidance. The story reminded me that underneath all of my struggle, and, as scared as I was, I could remember to lighten up and know that I belonged to something much bigger than myself.

Symbols don't have to be complicated or come from only dreams or visions. They are everywhere and can be used to uncover hidden meanings in very average settings.

I was working with a leadership team that was challenged with conflict and had problems with communication. While on a retreat, I asked the question, "What is it like to be part of this team?" Then I instructed the team members to spend some time outside and bring back an object that caught their attention. Everyone chose something and then came inside. One at a time they were asked to talk about the object they had chosen and, when finished, to place it in the center of the circle. They didn't have to know why they picked their object or come up with any deep meaning; they were just instructed to talk about it.

One quiet man, troubled by some unresolved issues around conflict within the leadership team, spoke up after he placed down a piece of dried, chewing gum. He said simply, "I'm not sure why this attracted my attention—I just know it's sticky." Initially, there was awkward laughter in the room, but as he went on to explain, everyone listened as he talked honestly about the difficulty he felt from the unresolved conflict and the way it had changed his view of coming to work.

Others placed additional objects that further revealed the effect of the team's communication breakdown, and the group began to talk and listen to each other in a respectful and sincere manner. They felt something shift, and people began talking to one another in more open ways. It wasn't long before they were able to clear up misunderstandings and move on in their work together.

This is the power behind symbols. They make visible what you know at some level but may not be conscious of right then. Once you can see it and know it, then you can do something different.

What are some other ways to discern? One way is through the body and your emotions.

Kinesiology is the study of the muscles and their

movements. It has been demonstrated that beneficial thoughts increase the strength of certain muscles, whereas negative thoughts weaken them. This means that you can use your body for the purpose of discerning. What strengthens your body is good and true for you and what weakens it is not. Test this for yourself by extending your arm and saying an untruth. Have someone push down on your arm as you do this and notice the weakness. Then say a truth and notice what happens.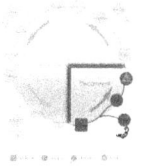

The way your heart feels offers another way to tap into wisdom. When you see, hear, or feel something that rings true for you, it may resonate in your heart like a ringing bell or cause your heart to flutter or feel spacious and open. When something is not true, you may feel a constriction, heaviness, or closing down. Think about some of the terms that we use frequently, such as "that fills my heart" or "my heart is about to burst," as well as "my heart is breaking" or "I have a heavy heart."

Using your mind to discern can be as simple as asking yourself, *Is this true? Is this for my highest and best good?* And then listen for the answer. If something doesn't feel right, ask again, and even a third time. Pay attention. Do you feel open and spacious? That will signal a "yes" answer. With a "no," you will feel a tightening, a constriction, or a stupor-like feeling.

I encourage you to experiment and try new ways of connecting to your own wisdom. You will discover a deeper sense of wholeheartedness, clarity and power.

Obstacle: Fear

In this third quadrant of Discernment, if you find that rather than feeling a sense of clarity and trust, you are feeling anxious and afraid and are second-guessing yourself, you may be in the obstacle of fear.

Vacationing one summer at a mountain resort, I watched a young mother walking with her son. He looked about four years old. They came to some stairs, and as the mother walked down the steps, she held her son's hand as he continued walking slightly above her on the level ground. The little boy came to a stop when he realized he was about five feet above his mother. She reached up her arms toward him and said, "Jump!"

I could see that their fingers were only inches apart, yet the little boy looked down at the distance to the ground and saw that jagged rocks faced outward and shook his head 'No.' "Come on," his mother said. "I'll catch you." He was having nothing to do with this. After a bit more persistence, the mother managed to catch her young son's fingers and gently pulled him closer to the edge. "I'm right here. Come on. Jump," she said. With no way out, he whimpered a weak 'Okay' and stopped resisting, but rather than jumping, he slumped down and became limp. His mom pulled him toward her, but with his weight heavy, on the way down he scrapped his knee on the rocks. His mother caught him, but he began to howl as she pulled him close. "Why didn't you jump?" she asked. "I did," he said, "but the rocks were bigger than you." He buried his head in her neck, while holding his knee tightly.

As I watching this scene unfold, I understood that little boy and thought how easy it is to let fear stop us.

What is fear? As Yann Martel writes in *The Story of Pi*, "I must say a word about fear. It is life's only true opponent. Only fear can defeat life… It goes for your weakest spot, which it finds with erring ease. It begins in your mind, always."

"Fear begins in your mind always," Martel writes. Think about that statement. How could you be afraid of something if you didn't think about it? Our thoughts begin in the mind and translate to the body. To live, fear must be fed, and it is fed by the attention we give it. As mentioned earlier, what we put attention on grows. The more we dwell on fear the more space it takes up in our inner world.

Once fear starts to build, it's difficult to extinguish. Fear thoughts feed one another, and the cycle can grow quickly from a small fire of cautious concerns and worry to a forest blaze. The thoughts can come from within you, be planted by the outside from 'well- meaning' individuals, or through any number of avenues such as the news or neighborhood gossip. Before you know it, they are firmly entrenched, the blaze is raging, and you are anxious, hyperactive, and doing your best to distract yourself with food, drink, sex, or endless activity.

Fear is a master of disguise. Anxiety, worry, timidness, nervousness and hesitancy are all parts of its wardrobe. It can create confusion, self-doubt, and feelings of isolation. Its purpose is the opposite of trust, and it keeps you from living life fully.

Of course, there are times when fear is necessary. It warns

you of danger, and as a built in protective mechanism, it supports your life. However, the purpose of fear is to warn you of danger, not to limit your living.

The 1900's French critic and poet, Guillaume Apollinaire, was known for exploring the inner world through his poetry. He wrote about the difficulty that arises when you step out to experience or achieve something new in your life. In this poem he speaks to the fear that is part of that process.

"Come the edge" he said. "No," they said.
"Come to the edge" he said.
"No," they replied. "Come to the edge" he said.
They came. He pushed them and they flew.

Guillaume Apollinaire

Change, uncertainty, and transitions all take you right to the edge. How easy to refuse the invitation: to push back, cling to what was, find a hiding place anywhere but close to that edge. Yet, there is no escape really. Eventually you get pushed or pulled off, just like that young boy in the mountains, even though you may yell the whole way down.

Apollinaire's poem refers to an edge. What happens at the edge that doesn't happen in other places? It's a place you go not just to be uncomfortable but rather to take an action so you can create different results. That means that the action you take has to be different from the ones that you normally take. That is the requirement of standing on the edge. It's asking you to step away from what is familiar and into the unknown—to develop a relationship with the unknown and uncertainty that is based in love, not fear.

There is a postcard of a group of people diving off four different diving boards into an old-fashioned pool. The photographer has caught them in midair with his shot. One man looks pained as he extends his arms out, and his body is stiff. Another is 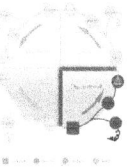 looking toward the camera, a jokester, making a face and pulling his legs up. There is a woman in a beautiful, open-hearted swan dive, and, off in the corner of the photo, is a slight-sized man who waits on the board with his fingers up to his mouth, chewing his nails. Each one is approaching the jump in a unique way.

The human condition often wants to know exactly where we will land, and *then* we will jump. But that is not the way of this world of trust. Instead, be willing to step out, even though the next step is not clear, and trust that you are supported by life itself. But you don't step out blindly; you step out in trust, led by your own wisdom.

Is the habit of being in fear something you struggle with? As long as you are alive and growing, you will have a relationship with fear. How big a role fear plays in your life will depend on how much you feed it. How long fear stays around will depend on your courage to call it by name and take steps to move through it. Each time you face your fear and choose trust, you establish a new habit for yourself.

*Serving others is one the fastest way I know to move from fear to trust. It will take you out of the downward, self-absorbed spiral of fear into a spacious place in your heart. Other ways to shift out of fear include getting exercise, being in nature, or listening to uplifting music. You can also reach out for help and let others know that you are afraid. They can come up with creative ideas or

offer helpful support. Use fear to generate movement and action to absorb anxiety.

 Result: Clarity

The result you are looking for with this quadrant of Discernment is clarity and a decision.

Clarity brings with it a sense of resolve, increased energy, and a feeling of relief. Even if the answer that comes is not the one you had hoped for, at least you know. You are free to make your decision.

Clarity is different from an insight, which is rarely strong enough to move you into action, as you can have a number of insights but still not have clarity. Instead, clarity comes with a sense of knowing. It's a feeling of certainty from within that often is hard to put into words. You just *know* and there is an inner resolve. Even if you wanted to go backward and play longer in an unproductive drama, it would not be as satisfying, because *now you know*. You have clarity on what needs to happen next.

Rebecca was a highly placed executive in a well-known company. She had worked hard and given up many weekends to achieve the respect and the salary she was earning. Her young son rarely got to see her because of her schedule. Over the year we worked she told me about issues that had come up at work that had her questioning whether this was the right job for her. She was proud to be in a leadership position and didn't want to disappoint others. But she sometimes wondered if her efforts were truly appreciated and if she was on the right path. She decided to pay closer attention to make sure that she was in the right position and company.

A large project was due and Rebecca put her heart and soul and a lot of time into completing it. She made sure everything was double-checked and hand delivered the final product to her boss on the weekend. She 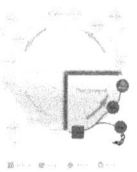 missed her son's school play and missed sleep but felt she had done her best. The project was well received. So Rebecca was stunned when soon thereafter she had a disappointing performance review. Rather than being recognized and acknowledged for all the work she had done, she received below average marks in effort put forth and as a team player. Surprised and disappointed, she stepped back and took time to reflect. It was during this time of reflection that clarity came. *She was not appreciated.* She had felt unappreciated and undervalued at her work for a long time. She'd always been able to justify the lack of recognition to herself. But now she knew. It was time to go. Before, she had gone back and forth with herself, but after the performance review she said there was no longer any doubt and that it was time to act. What surprised her was the calmness she felt with the certainty. She quit her job, took some time to refocus, and started a business with her brother that they had dreamed about for years.

Sometimes you may get clear, but because it is not the answer you wanted or expected, you may not act on it, and instead find yourself in confusion. That happened to Dan, a personal trainer, who had a strong sense of trust in himself and yet became confused because of conflicting interests.

Dan had been working for a year when he decided to bring in a few people to help him grow his business. Skilled in body mechanics, conditioning, and weight training, he wanted to work with colleagues who had different skills sets, so long as they shared his values of being fit themselves, of caring about people, and of having integrity.

He placed an ad, and a few days later as he read Sally's resume, he was impressed and thought he might have found his first trainer. Dan's first hint that something was not right came when he introduced himself as Dan and she called him Daniel. He said it was something about the way she used Daniel instead of Dan that didn't feel right, but he brushed it off, thinking he was too critical.

They set up an appointment, but a day before they were to meet, Sally called and said something had come up and she needed to reschedule. They set another time but on that day she didn't show. There was no call or e-mail from her explaining what had happened. Dan thought it himself, "Well, that says it all," and put his attention toward other applicants.

Two weeks later Sally called, apologizing effusively. She said an emergency had come up, and she was so sorry. She asked him if they could please meet. At first he said no, but she was so insistent and apologetic about the incident that he agreed to meet two days later.

On that day, while Dan was working with a client, Sally showed up two hours early. She said she was in the area and thought she'd just drop by. Surprised and taken aback, Dan explained that he was busy with a client but that he was available later as agreed upon. As she left, Dan noticed once again that something didn't feel quite right.

When they finally met, Dan discovered that Sally had everything he wanted in a trainer, so he began to rethink

Discernment

his decision. At the end of the interview, he casually asked her what it was that kept her from their previously scheduled meeting two weeks ago. She said that she and her husband were suing his family over some unresolved issues that had been going on for quite a while and made some critical comments about her in-laws. Dan thanked her for her time, and she left.

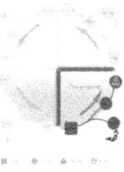

Dan found himself unsure of what to do next. Red flags were going up, and yet he was very impressed with her appearance and resume. Also, he needed to get someone in to help with the expenses. He and his wife had a two-year-old and a new baby and living on one salary was challenging.

We met that morning and talked about the situation. I asked Dan if Sally's actions reflected the personal values he lives by. "No," he said. I asked him to reflect on the impressions he had on the first phone call. He talked about how something was triggered when she didn't call him by the name he had used to introduce himself. That was his first insight. He also noted how he had discounted it. That's not uncommon. Luckily, if something is important, it will continue to come up if we're willing to listen.

I asked him if there were any other insights or impressions. He mentioned her not calling back after missing an appointment and showing up at the wrong time. "I knew something was off, but I thought we all make mistakes, and I wanted to give her a chance," he said. Another insight came at the end of the meeting when Sally explained that they were suing her husband's family. Dan is part of a close-knit family that cares deeply about one other. The idea of suing someone in his own family would never cross

Dan's mind, so when Sally mentioned this point, he felt a tightening in his body.

So what was the problem? Why was there confusion for Dan in coming to a decision? Dan had a financial need and wanted to fill the space. His will got in the way of listening to his deeper wisdom. He had received clarity but had brushed it aside. Once Dan was able to reconnect to his vision and his values, take a step back, and reflect, clarity returned. This time he took action. He called Sally, thanked her, and told her he didn't see it working out. He then put his attention to other candidates. It wasn't long before he found a much better fit and was closer to creating his vision of a fully staffed wellness center.

This happens a lot. We get a feeling something isn't quite right, but because of outside circumstances choose to ignore it. Or we don't like the answer that is showing up and want a different one. We have free will, and so we always have a choice, but that does not necessarily bring us a sense of inner calm. Confusion is more often the outcome.

Once there is clarity, action must follow. If you get clear and know what you need to do, but don't do it, you will end up frustrated and, weaken your sense of trust in your own wisdom. Many people excel in the area of analyzing and become hooked on the figuring-out process, but then drop the ball when it's time to take action. I understand this. I did it for years. I would have insights and know what to do; I would talk about it, plan it out, and yet not do it. I dropped the ball and, consequently, missed many opportunities to strengthen my own sense of resolve. Energy can be tied up for years in this drama of perfection, over analysis, and nonaction. Clarity without action is fantasy. Taking action on clarity is what will increase your confidence in your own wisdom and create a sense of flow in your life.

Once you have clarity, but before you take action, take a few minutes to write down the process of how you got there. This will help build your confidence in your Self and give you something to look back on at a later date.

Once clear, be bold and move into the next quadrant of Action. Remember when you align with your inner guidance you are aligned with the unlimited power of life's mystery. If you stay in harmony and aligned with your inner wisdom, that spiritual force will go to work on your behalf as you take action.

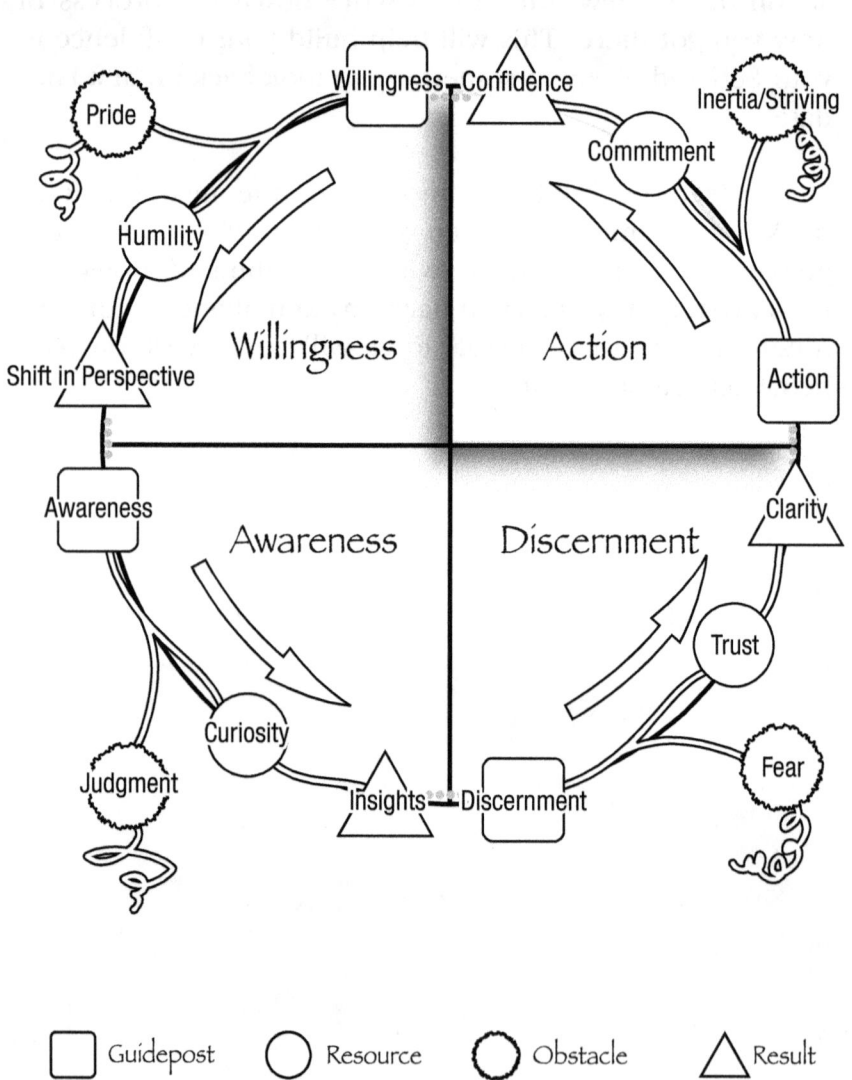

CHAPTER SEVEN

Action

Will you take action?

*"Tell me, what will you do with
your one wild and precious life?"*

Mary Oliver

I can remember the first time I rode a bike on my own and the thrill of riding down my street, pumping the pedals, and feeling the wind against my face. I still love to ride, so the exhibit at the Science Museum that demonstrates how the muscles in our legs work together to enable us to ride a bike, quickly captured my attention.

In a glassed display is a model of half of a body from the hips down. It is sitting on a bike and set up so that children, young and old, can push one of four buttons to activate the muscles on the legs to move the pedals on the bike. If you push a button to constrict the right quadriceps, the right leg moves up. To "ride" the bike, the other leg must be worked as well, so then you push the button that constricts the left quadriceps. There are more buttons and more muscles to work with, but the idea is that all muscles must work together to pedal the bike and get forward action. If you're skillful, it is not long before both legs are moving in tandem – a beautiful sight! If you are not, it is forever hopeless trying to coordinate these movements as the muscles and buttons work against each other.

While I waited my turn, I had time to watch people of all ages work with the buttons. Some never got it – they got frustrated and gave up. Others would try a bit, laugh at their efforts, and move on after a short time. What fun it was to watch one young boy, about 11, sit down and within a few short minutes, create a flow that was seamless. We all stood mesmerized and watched the give and take, extend and contract, work and rest rhythm that he masterfully produced. There was effort, but also no effort, and it was marvelous to watch.

Balanced action has a sense of flow. It is a combination of effort and effortlessness. You use your will as you actively engage in action, but you also let go and listen, intuitively knowing when to act and when to rest in order to most efficiently and effectively move forward.

In many ways, in these current times, we have lost this natural rhythm. It is easy to get caught in striving, struggling, and working endlessly to make things happen, all the while exhausting yourself and creating patterns of stress that wear you out. Listening with the 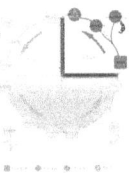 intent to be in partnership with your own Self connects you to a greater truth and allows you to once again flow in life in balanced action.

In this section, before we address the resources, obstacles, and results of the guidepost of Action, we'll explore two topics: taking responsibility and letting go of attachment to the outcome.

Taking Responsibility

Responsibility is doing what you say you will do. It is being accountable, dependable, and reliable. When you take responsibility for a choice, an outcome, or a dream, you step into what is possible with both feet and do what is necessary to achieve the results that you desire.

Obstacles will arise, doubts may seep in, worry may make you stumble, but when you take responsibility, you keep moving forward one step at a time. There are no little steps. Each step forward counts.

In his book *Servant Leader*, Robert Greenleaf writes about John Woolman, a man who devoted himself to eliminating slavery among the Quakers. Touched deeply by the injustice of slavery, he accomplished his goal—almost single handedly—by visiting and revisiting the slave holders along the East Coast, one by one, and respectfully asking them questions, not in a way that caused them to be defensive, but in a way that invited them to listen deeply to their own hearts. He asked questions such as, "What does the owning of slaves do to you as a moral, conscious person? What kind of a life are you passing down to your children?" Over a period of thirty years, his gentle, yet probing, approach allowed the Quakers to end slave ownership. Woolman's confidence in the goodness of others and his ability to act in alignment with his inner promptings was reflected in the results of his life's work. Because of his efforts, by 1770 (100 years before the Civil War) Quakers no longer held slaves.

What was it that helped Woolman continue year after year with his campaign? What kept him from becoming discouraged and quitting? It had to have been hard showing up at those farms when slavery was accepted and livelihoods depended on it. He was surely met with disbelief and anger. Yet, he took responsibility for what he believed in and, in doing so, he was given the strength and skills to remain committed, focused, and disciplined.

Few of us will be called on to live the life that Woolman did, but all of us will face the questions: Will you trust yourself, take responsibility and put in the time, energy, and focus required for the result you want?

Sometimes it's easier to take responsibility for others than for yourself. Lynn was 52 when she and her husband divorced. She had been a stay-at-home mom, active in her community, and had thought she'd be married for the rest of her life. With the divorce came many new challenges. She had to manage her money, work for the first time in twenty years, and figure out what she wanted to do with her life. So much of her life and energy had been spent

taking care of her husband, family, church and community – everyone and everything except for herself. She had neglected her own health and well-being.
She made the choice to take responsibility for herself. It was remarkable to see how her life changed when she did. She lost weight and moved into a home she could afford. She took an accounting class and rediscovered how much she enjoyed working with numbers. It took a few years, but she created a life that is vibrant, fun, and exactly what she wanted. It began when she chose to take the responsibility for herself and her well-being. Her own wisdom reminded her that in order to be there for others, she had to be there first for herself.

Letting Go of Attachment to the Outcome

My friend Ann and her husband John noticed a bird had built a nest in the low branches of their backyard tree. They watched as the mother bird sat on the egg and were delighted when a baby bird was born. Day after day, they would check on the progress of the little bird, noticing how big it was getting. One day though, they came home and saw the baby bird on the ground. Immediately, they worried that maybe the bird had broken its wing or that perhaps a cat was going to eat it. They thought about picking it up and putting it in a box but noticed that the mother was close by and so decided to wait. While recounting the story to a friend, and after giving a description of the bird, her friend said to her, "Don't worry. It's a Mockingbird. That is what Mockingbirds do. The babies spend a few weeks on the ground before they learn to fly." What a surprise! Ann had never heard of that and she realized that she had spent all this time and energy worrying and assuming that what had happened was a bad thing... yet, 'That is what Mockingbirds do'.

It's so easy to make the assumption that something is bad or good, yet so often we don't know.

There's an old Zen story that has been told and retold often. There was a man who lived long ago with his family in a rural community. One day his son was out exploring in the woods and found a horse. He brought it home. The neighbors, upon seeing the new horse, exclaimed to the man, "You are so lucky! Look at that, your son found a horse. You must be the most fortunate man in the village." The man listened and said, "Maybe."

The next day the son was riding the horse, was thrown off, and broke his leg. The neighbors, lamenting his situation, cried out, "How unfortunate for you! How horrible that your son, riding his horse, broke his leg. Now you have lost your help. How terrible." The man listened and again responded, "Maybe."

A week later, war broke out in the country and all able-bodied young men were forced to go and fight, all except the son whose leg was broken. Once again the neighbors came by and said, "You are so fortunate that your son will be allowed to remain. You are most lucky." Once again, the man said, "Maybe." And so the story goes, on and on.

We never really know, do we? Something happens that seems unbearable, and you wonder "Why me?" and question how you will ever deal with the situation. Yet later, with the benefit of hindsight, you may recognize the experience as a gift. There are so many stories of people expressing gratitude for an illness, a difficult childhood, or even a tragedy that at first seemed horrible and yet turned out to bring unexpected gifts.

Balanced action needs space for surprise, flexibility, and flow. When we get attached to something happening in a certain way, we miss opportunities. There is no space for what is possible because we are so focused on what we want.

Practice letting go of the attachment to the outcome with small things first then with more important decisions. This doesn't mean you don't care, rather you care from a neutral place. Instead of getting pulled into drama and emotional turmoil, you are able to step back and look at it more objectively.

An artist friend of mine doesn't know what is being created until it comes forth. She shows up with a general idea, listens, and acts on her promptings and does the work without judging it or over thinking. As soon as she starts to force her will or to resist what is wanting to come out, she thwarts her own process. She has learned how to enjoy and flow with the creative energy rather than trying to control it.

Michael, a successful painter and teacher, tells me that one reason he has so many projects going on at the same time is because it helps him stay less attached and more fluid. By painting six canvases at the same time, he finds himself more open to what shows up. He goes from painting to painting, noticing new elements to add or places that need a bit more color here or there, all the while listening deeply to his own instincts and promptings. He started doing this after finding himself stuck one too many times on a single painting. This method has helped him stay fluid and open to his creativity.

Being unattached to the outcome, yet open to what is possible, helps you become more tuned in to synchronicity, serendipity, and amazing opportunities. With detachment, you're able to pay attention and see more clearly when opportunities present themselves, and it is more fun.

Here are a few tips to help you stay unattached to the outcome and yet remain open to what is possible:

- Remember the words, "I don't know." Even if you think you know the best outcome, something even better may present itself. If what you want does not happen the way you wanted it, ask the question, "What is trying to happen here?"

- Pay attention to what is set in motion with your thoughts. Feeling tight and constricted? What are you thinking that is causing that feeling? Is it true?

- Keep an eye on the big picture, not the little ups and downs.

- Focus on what is working rather than what is not working.

- Release trying to be perfect, and aim for excellence instead.

- Become present. Let go of the past and future and be in the moment.

- Lighten up. Find the humor. Life is a lot more fun when you can enjoy it. Laughing is one of the best ways to regain equilibrium.

Try this. For one full day, approach people and situations as if you are expecting to see or hear something funny. Go about your day as if you were a comedian looking for new material. Rather than wait for something to amuse you, look for it. Notice how you approach new situations. At the end of the day notice how you feel. What did you learn?

 Resource: Commitment

The resource for this quadrant is commitment. It will keep you strong, expansive, and focused as you take action.

Commitment means to "give in trust." What is it that you are giving in trust? It is your word. When you commit, you give your word to do something; to put your efforts and resources behind keeping your promise.

Your word has power. Long ago, when a person gave his word, it was so highly regarded that it was considered legally binding. It was, and still is, the foundation for trust in relationships.

All commitments are personal and come from the heart. Commitments made only with the intellect may feel shallow or like drudgery. They will tire you out and have "no juice." But when you commit to something that is important, meaningful and real for you, it engages your heart, mind, and body, and you are energetically fed and renewed as you extend effort.

To build confidence and create more flow in your life, the commitment you make is to stay aligned with your own wisdom and be true to your Self. You give your word not to self-abandon but instead to listen to your truth and act on the clarity you receive.

When you commit to trusting your own wisdom, you align with forces greater than you can imagine and put unseen dynamics into motion. Along with your efforts of self-discipline, focus, and determination come results gained, effortlessly, through coincidence, luck, or fortuitous circumstances.

Nothing connects us with our personal power more than commitment. Aligned with the unlimited potential within, the opportunities for productive action are endless.

Entelechy (En-tell-a-key) is a word that was coined by Aristotle. It means *your greatest potential actualized*. For example, the entelechy of an acorn is an oak tree. The belief is that within the acorn is everything it needs to become what it is meant to become. Information encoded within the acorn guides its growth and development toward being its best and organically bringing out what is possible. Of course, for the acorn, other factors contribute – water, sunlight, location – but the acorn has within itself the way to grow into its "best self" and actualize its potential.

Your inner wisdom, your True Self, knows what is possible for you at your very best and guides you towards your actualization. You will recognize when you are living in your truth and doing what you were meant to do by the increase of confidence, enthusiasm, and freedom you feel.

The ability to commit is greatly influenced by our habits. You can have the desire to do something truly wonderful, something of great vision and value, but if your habits do not support you in a healthy way, it is difficult to achieve the dream.

A habit is simply a disposition or tendency to act in a certain way. We all have thousands of habits that help us in our daily lives. If we had to stop and relearn each time we wanted to shower, brush our teeth, drive, or pay our bills, life would be difficult and we'd waste a lot of energy and effort that could be better used elsewhere. Positive habits help us to operate on autopilot so we don't have to learn the same things over and over again. Our habits are grounded in our beliefs, and we all have both empowering and disempowering beliefs.

Sitting with Larry at lunch, I was struck by how relaxed and open he always was. It seemed that regardless of circumstances, Larry had developed a way to enjoy and flow with life's ups and downs. He told me that he had taught technology classes at a university for ten years and assumed that he would finish his career teaching. But when it came time for him to receive tenure, it was denied. Telling that story, without any sort of regret or bitterness, he recounted how he was disappointed, but also how once he realized that there was no longer a future for him in teaching, he decided to start his own consulting business. I said to him, "It seems as though you weren't too upset about not getting tenure after all those years of teaching. How did you handle that?" He said, "You know, I didn't worry about it. I was born under a lucky star. Things always seem to work out."

Imagine having the belief that you were born under a lucky star! How would you react when unexpected or unplanned events happen? Anyone who knows Larry would agree that his own hard work created his luck, but in his mind he perceives he was born lucky and, consequently, approaches challenges with an open mind and confidence based on this deeply held belief and perception.

Disempowering perceptions or old stories we tell ourselves about our insufficiencies, on the other hand, keep us stuck in patterns of weakness, victimization, self-judgment, indulgence, and hiding. Like weeds in a garden, it's not enough to cut off the top because the roots go down deep into the subconscious mind. Instead, you have to be willing to get to the core issue and put energy behind a new perception. For a transformation to occur there must be a change in the way we think.

These perceptions and old tired, worn out stories reside in the mind, and yet changing them requires engaging the heart. When we have a limiting perception, we believe it. That is why we live from it because we believe it is the truth. There may be some small truth connected to a limiting belief, but it's not a full truth.

For example, you could say, "People can't be trusted because they can never be counted on." There is truth in that. Many times people do not do what they say they will do. But it's not the whole truth. People also can love us, care for us and be there for us. When we get fixated on one "truth" and ignore the other possible truths, we create limits for ourselves. Using the above example, we can create a life that is based on distrust of others and experience the loneliness that comes with depending only on ourselves.

Out of all the perceptions we have, the ones that we believe about ourselves personally are the most important to examine. How you choose to see yourself determines much about what you will allow into your life, how you will take action, and how much you trust yourself. The choice to see yourself as whole, powerful, and "enough" is yours. It may not have been earlier—when  you were very young and seeds of insufficiency, distrust, fear, or doubt may have been planted and watered within your psyche—but it's never too late to see with fresh eyes, and it's never too late to uncover limiting beliefs, recognize them for what they are, and choose healthy empowering beliefs to live by.

Commitment is the key to experiencing your true power.

When you commit to living from your own wisdom, your true Self, not only are you supported, but all of life is supported as you realize your potential.

In Chapter 9 there are exercises that will help you uncover and change limiting beliefs, as well as other ideas to increase your ability to take action.

 ## Obstacles: Inertia and/or Over Striving

If you find that rather than moving forward, you are feeling stuck or scattered, it may be that you are caught in the challenge of inertia or over striving. Inertia is being stuck, passive, disengaged, or unable to motivate yourself to act. The other, over striving, is characterized by intense, forceful, or overzealous behavior. Both are about trying to control an outcome rather than learning to trust and act in partnership with our own wisdom.

During times of transition, change, and uncertainty, these obstacles can be a wake up call to help you remember to choose wisely where to put your attention.

The first of the obstacles is inertia.

Linda, an accomplished businesswoman, had spent her high school and college years in a variety of countries. She was no stranger to change and transition, and, in fact, usually welcomed it. Now though, at age 47, she found herself in a new place. Her most recent job had been a disappointment, and after a tense and difficult situation, she and her supervisor decided it was best for all if Linda left the company. She found herself frozen in fear and feeling lost. Rather than searching for a new job, she watched TV and distracted herself with the internet. "In my heart I've known for the last year that this job wasn't right, and yet I stayed on because I didn't know what else to do," she said. Linda knew she was stuck and was frustrated at her own resistance. Now the decision was being forced on her, and she was afraid.

Inertia can feel like you are being weighted down. Sluggish, heavy, and uninspired, you may feel overwhelmed by the magnitude of what is needed. You don't feel up to the job and often resent suggestions, ideas, or encouragement. It's easy to become discouraged and depressed when in inertia. This is the obstacle that has people getting into bed, pulling the sheets over their faces, and wanting everyone to leave them alone and everything to go away. Often feelings, such as life is not fair, come up along with being bored, weak, and feeling powerless. Sometimes there is an intense desire for food, sugar, shopping, or alcohol. These are used to further numb thoughts and feelings. The illusion is that somehow we can make it go away by distractions. Of

course, all that does is prolong the inertia. Linda was self-observant, realized she couldn't do it alone, and so she reached out for help. Friends offered to exercise with her. She met with a head hunter, updated her resume and made sure she was accountable to a small group of professionals. She discovered that she wanted to make a big change. Her heart was no longer in the work she had been doing for the last twenty years. She wanted to start her own company. When she became clear about what she really wanted, she was inspired, and her creativity began to flow. A year later, even after a rocky launch, she was fully engaged and enthusiastic about her clients and work.

You know you are in inertia when you procrastinate, become a perfectionist, go into denial, feel victimized, sabotage yourself, give in to distractions, or find yourself talking about what you are going to do rather than doing it. Rather than judging yourself harshly, simply recognize where you are and be willing to step back so you can gain a new perspective. Be curious and listen for clarity. Reconnect with what is most important to you, and then recommit to balanced action.

There are many different ways to get out of inertia. Here are some of my favorites.

- Go back and trace your steps to how you made your original commitment. Then recommit.

- Do something. It doesn't matter how small the action is; just do something that will get you going.

- Ask for help, either from a professional or from your

friends, family, or colleagues. When our confidence and personal power hit bottom, another person's acknowledgment of our capabilities can make all the difference.

- Get physical. Walk, dance, jump, hike, do yoga, stretch – move your body.

- Give yourself the benefit of the doubt. Ask: What am I afraid of? What inspires me right now? What is in the way of my enthusiasm?

- Explore whether there is a limiting belief at the root of the inertia. Write a new empowering belief.

- Find a book, lecture, or tape that speaks to your problem or that inspires you. Visit a bookstore or library and browse through the shelves. Pick the books that catch your attention.

- Watch your diet. Food can easily be used to sabotage and distract. Chocolate, caffeine, alcohol, sugar, and overeating can all play a role in adding to this type of inertia. I know immediately when I get caught in inertia because I will get into the sweets. What about you?

- Break down a task into small pieces. Do one thing. Notice if you find yourself blaming or being overly harsh with yourself or others. Learn what you need to learn, and then let it go. No need to waste time and energy with regrets, over thinking, or over analyzing.

The other obstacle in this quadrant of action is over striving.

Over striving is the opposite of inertia. This obstacle sounds something like this. "If I don't push, shove, or force myself, nothing will happen."

Over striving is a form of willfulness that is seen as intensity, bullheadedness, lack of awareness, or overzealousness. It's like being given the go ahead to take two steps and instead running five miles down the road. What we missed after the two steps was that we were supposed to take the next right turn. It's hard to listen to your true Self when the drive and excitement of taking action is so strong that sometimes it takes on a life of its own.

In this case, as with inertia, there is a disconnect and a lack of consciousness. The will is engaged behind the personality or adapted self rather than the true Self. We are no longer in partnership and are not paying attention to our own wisest self.

I had an experience with this type of energy that I will never forget. I enjoy the opportunity to meet new people and collaborate. When I first started my career, I was invited by a good friend to meet with some colleagues who wanted to develop a new project. I was so excited to be included in this group, which I held in high regard, that my mind raced forward, and I found myself mentally planning on all of us working together and eventually even sharing their office space! It was in this state of excitement that I went to the meeting. For the first thirty minutes it went well enough, but in the discussion, we began to talk about the project, or rather I began to talk about the project and went on and on in my excitement about all the ways I saw this unfolding. I remember it made such sense to me. I could see it all clearly and couldn't wait to share it, but it felt intense, and it was hard for me to stop talking and difficult to listen to what others were saying. I left the meeting feeling a bit dazed, and I'm sure they felt it as well. Later my friend asked me what had happened. Sheepishly, I apologized for my behavior, but I truthfully didn't understand myself where the intensity had come from. I was embarrassed and, of course, lost an opportunity as they never did call back to continue the conversation. It was a few years later as I studied more about energy that I realized what had happened. I had abandoned my true Self and instead aligned with my ego or adapted self; it was all about me. After that experience, I dutifully watched the way I prepared for other meetings! It was embarrassing but it helped me to understand the false sense of power that can come with overstriving.

My example was one way over striving can show up in life, but this kind of disconnection can be seen in many situations, specifically, in people who are working hard to make things happen but are exhausted or worn out. They often take responsibility for everyone at their own expense. It's the sister who keeps everyone on task, worried about each sibling, and yet neglecting her own health and well-being. It's the business owner who says he wants to create a team but finds it next to impossible to delegate and has to show up at every meeting "just to make sure" it all goes well. It's the manager who says he wants to have collaboration but puts all of his time into micromanaging others and never gets his own work done. All of these are examples of over striving – pushing and forcing our will rather than listening to and trusting our inner guidance and moving in partnership with it.

Over striving, aside from slowing down the flow and ease

of taking action, taxes our health and well-being.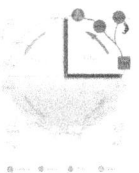

Are you over striving?

Are you pushing to make everything happen and driving hard while frustrated that things aren't going fast enough? Are you staying up too late? Do you want to just get this thing finished? Do you feel rushed and hurried with no time for anything? Do you get frustrated that others just don't get it?

What will help you come back into the flow of trust when you are caught in over striving?

- Stop. Whatever you have to do, just stop speaking, moving, and doing.

- Breathe and make a conscious choice to let go.

- Remember respect. Over striving is disrespectful to yourself and others.

- Do either a sitting- or standing-forward bend. If standing, bend at the waist and let your arms hang down. If sitting, extend your arms over your legs. These are poses of humility, and they will help slow you down and quiet your mind.

- Become present. See the beauty around you. Let it bring you into the present moment.

- Think up at least three other possible perspectives on whatever it is you are working on.

- What is it that you really want to have happen? Go back to your original intention and ask yourself if there is a better way to engage others and yourself at this time. Do you want to be right or connect?

- Be kind toward yourself. If you are striving, chances are that after realizing it you may feel unsettled or embarrassed. Acknowledge it, and then let go.

How do you find the way to decisive, committed action and yet stay open, flexible, and allow for the flow and ease of the work? It's found through trial and error, practice, and developing the skills to sense when you are in alignment and when you're not.

Result: Confidence, Expansiveness and Flow.

The final result of this pathway is the expansive, open state of confidence and flow that comes when you are in alignment with your true Self and in balanced action.

The more aligned and in action we are with our own wisdom, the more we can relax into the flow of life, and what is most important gets done.

The resources of humility, curiosity, trust, and commitment create the positive energy that allows you to open what is possible and be well supported. When you trust your own wisdom, your true Self, you tap into your greatest potential for innovation, problem solving and productivity. You awaken and unleash *your* gifts, skills and talents. Think of it as an upward spiral, open and expansive.

Confidence based on Self trust doesn't mean that you are free from doubts, negative thoughts, or uncomfortable feelings. Rather it means that, despite those voices, you know how to listen for the truth. This calms us down, and lets us live life in a way that promotes self-acceptance and allows the full expression of love to emerge. During times of transitions, change, and uncertainty, this foundation of trust helps you to navigate in a secure and connected way so that you are able to make connections and discover possibilities rather than get lost in the fear, worry, or self-doubt.

Confidence comes from "doing": stepping out, falling down, getting up, falling down again, and getting up again and so on. It is in the doing that we grow and experience our own power as individuals. Waiting for ideal circumstances before taking action is rarely an option available to us. Confidence is built in the real world where you take real risks, winning some and losing some, but all the while showing up and acting on what you are prompted to do. In doing this you develop a sense of your own truth, fine tuning signals, sensations, promptings, and your instinctual wisdom.

Confidence can come from a leap of faith but more often it consists of small, manageable, self-disciplined steps. You learn to count on your Self, keep the promises you make to your Self, and depend on the partnership of co-creation.

As you grow in confidence and Self trust, your ability to speak out with your unique voice—verbally or through other expressions—grows as well. Your voice reflects how you take a stand in the world. If there is an internal imbalance, it's often reflected in the voice as sounding strained, dry, forced, or wishy-washy. There is a lack of congruency.

Where we put our attention while we are speaking creates an energy. Our voice reflects the quality of our attention. As you grow in confidence and trust, your ability to speak out in the world grows and fear lessens. Your voice then becomes an offering, and your promptings a responsibility to share.

Public speaking is terrifying to many people. It ranks higher on the scale of fear factors than death. What is it that is so unsettling about standing up and speaking in front of others? Why does it take so much courage to express ourselves in front of others in an authentic, heartfelt way? And what would be needed in order to make the experience one of connectedness and sharing instead of fear and dread?

> *"Just as the eyes are the mirror of the soul, so too is the voice a clear reflection of the heart. The whole body is an instrument moving on the circular flow and interconnectedness of the breath. In this way the vehicle of voice allows the unique resonance of each individual's inner self to be expressed and experienced. Through the gift of the voice, we can align with the wholeness naturally within and then freely extend our inner vibration outward, creating a deeper connection within and around us."*
>
> Meg Byerlein

We are always vulnerable to judgment and criticism from

others when we speak out. Many of us hold back what we know to be true in order not to draw attention to ourselves, not to make waves, and to stay instead in the background. But your voice is important and your perspective adds much to conversations and 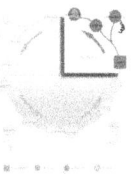 dialogue. You certainly do not have the only answer, but you have *your answer* and it's yours to share. When you are able to say what is true for you, people listen, not just with their ears, but also with their hearts and minds. They pay attention to your body language and can sense truth.

Throughout time, there has been great emphasis on the power of the word, both negative and positive. A curse spoken with conviction to another has been known to cripple the person on the receiving end of it. Words of loving kindness have been known to bless and heal. When you speak with your authentic voice from your true Self, you bring what is within—in terms of your heart, knowledge and wisdom—out for others to experience. When you act on what is within, as the poet Emerson says, "miracles happen".

Each time you keep the promises you make and do what you stay you will do and don't do what you say you will not do, you deepen and strengthen Self trust. As change, transitions and uncertainty arise you are able to meet them from a place of confidence, ease and flow.

It all begins with willingness…..

the art & practice of trust

CHAPTER EIGHT

A Final Note......

As long as we are alive and growing we will always come up against challenges that take us into new territory. Sometimes it will be our choice. Other times it will be the consequences of our choices or something that happened that was totally out of our control. The constant is that it is new territory; it is unfamiliar, unknown and we have never been there before. This can bring up worry, self doubt and fear and if we perceive that the stakes are high, these emotions can confuse, distract or immobilize us.

But there are other possibilities. New territory can be exciting, adventurous, filled with unlimited opportunities. We can navigate through this new space in a way that allows us to stay open, flexible and awake to what is possible. We can trust our true Self and depend, rely and count on our own wisdom to guide us so that rather than getting tied up in the struggle we can grow and experience the strength and connection inherent in life.

As we deepen our Self trust it creates the freedom to strengthen and build relationships with others so that our circle of influence widens and we shift from independent thinking to interdependence; the greatest value of all. Interdependence gives us the power to tap into a collective wisdom and create and problem solve at the highest levels.

Each one of us has something unique and valuable to offer that is ours alone to share. If fear dominates, we will be constricted and limited in all that we do, but if we are willing to widen our perspective, be curious and step out in trust, we will discover not only the power and courage to take our next steps but endless possibility and boundless opportunity.

CHAPTER NINE

Practices for the Four Quadrants

Willingness
Task: To create space
Question: *Are you willing?*
Resource: Humility
Obstacle: Pride
Result: Shift in Perspective

Discernment
The task: To decide
Question: *Will you trust your Self?*
Resource: Trust
Obstacle: Fear
Result: Clarity

Awareness
Task: To gather information
Question: *Will you pay attention?*
Resource: Curiosity
Obstacle: Judgment
Result: Insights

Action
The task: To take action
Question: *Will you take action?*
Resource: Commitment
Obstacle: Inertia/Over striving
Result: Confidence, expansiveness, and flow

1. This path is counter-intuitive and goes counter clockwise on purpose. It's normal to tighten up and constrict the heart, mind and body when going through a place of uncertainty. The first thing you are asked you to do is open up and create space so that you can shift your perspective. It's common to feel resistance but important to become expansive in order to broaden your perspective.

2. Take a moment and reflect on the challenge that you are facing. Write it down. Start with the intention to widen your perspective. Realize that in the constricted state of fear, doubt or worry your options for creativity and problem solving are limited. Create space. Open up and remember that you are not alone in this. You are part of something much greater than yourself and if you chose to broaden, widen and find space it will help you

move forward. Are you seeing something from a limited perspective? Come up with four other ways to view the situation.

Next pay attention. Let yourself be curious. Ask yourself, "What is the question that, if I had the answer, it would help me move forward? And then be patient and listen for insights. No acting needy or rushing. Allow yourself the time you need to pay attention to what is meaningful and has heart for you.

When you are ready to make a decision and choose your next steps, trust your Self. Stay open, relaxed and use the wisdom of your heart, mind and body. Align with trust rather than old patterns of doubt, fear and anxiety. Be courageous and look for both the tangible and intangible ways that life shows up to help you move forward. Wait for clarity.

Then act decisively. Commit to doing what you are prompted to do. The first step out into the unknown is often unsettling. Do it anyway. Trust what comes up for you and act on it. Then pay attention to what is next. Stay open, flexible and present.

The resources of humility, curiosity, trust and the commitment to be true to yourself will create a container that will support you as you take your next steps.

3. When feeling off or disconnected, identify the obstacle you are caught in and then use the resource from the prior quadrant to help you reconnect. For example, if you are caught in fear, go back to the resource of the prior quadrant. In this case, you would go back

to awareness and the resource of curiosity. It is very difficult to move into trust while caught in the midst of fear. Instead, if you go back to the prior guidepost and use that resource, it will help you reconnect with your truth. Ask yourself questions to gain insights. If that is not enough, go back to the quadrant of willingness and the resource of humility in order to quell your fear.

4. If you jump ahead into action before you have clarity, you will probably end up in inertia or over striving. Make sure that you have received clarity before taking action so that you can stay open and receptive to opportunities. Insights are exciting but it is with clarity that you will have a sense of resolve or 'knowing.'

5. You will likely encounter the greatest tension in the quadrants of awareness and discernment. In awareness, be willing to hear or observe things about your situation, yourself, and others that may not be pleasant. With discernment, be willing to hold the tension inherent in uncertainty until you have inner confirmation and clarity. Both require patience, but like any new skill, the more experience you have the easier it becomes.

Practices for Each Quadrant

Willingness

Fear, doubt, and worry constrict our minds, hearts, and bodies. The practices for this quadrant are focused on relaxing your body, opening up your mind, and creating space in your heart, so that you can shift your perspective.

Do a practice. Spend quiet time with yourself each day. I started a practice by committing to taking five minutes each morning. All I did was find a place where I would not be disturbed and practiced breathing. After a few days, I noticed that throughout my day I felt more open and happier, so I increased it and then added five minutes of sitting in silence, not from guilt or a feeling that I should, but because it made me feel better. Eventually, work your way up to sitting quietly for twenty minutes a day. Notice the way you feel and act on the days that you take the time to practice.

Open up with exercise. Millions of people begin their day with exercise. Qigong, yoga, running, a brisk walk with the dog, you name it. Exercise gets energy moving and shifting in the body, and the extra blood flow helps the mind to awaken and clear. Creating space in the body through movement and breathing helps relax the mind.

Breathe. Begin to pay attention to your breath. Without changing it, pay attention to how you are breathing. Close your eyes. Take a few moments and notice as the breath comes in and out of your body.

As you inhale, feel the rise of your belly, and as you exhale, feel the release. Release your shoulders and soften your face. If you find it hard to release the breath into the belly, think of something pleasant and gently invite yourself to soften and let the muscles of your stomach relax. If you like to visualize, think of dropping a penny down a well as you drop your breath deeper into your belly. Close your eyes and practice breathing like this for ten breaths.

The breath is the bridge between the heart, mind, and body. When you drop the breath down into the body and feel the rise of the belly as you inhale, you are signaling to the body it can relax. Breathing like this creates space and quiets the mind.

Sometimes people feel uncomfortable as they practice this breathing exercise. If so, take it slowly. You might try practicing this as you walk outside, or lie down with a telephone book on your belly to help you focus on this new way to breathe. It's natural as we learn new skills to feel apprehension or resistance. Recognize it briefly, but continue on.

Conscious Breathing. Take a seat and place your feet flat on the floor, legs uncrossed, and spine lengthened. Draw your attention to your breath, and notice where you feel the breath first come into your body. Trace the breath as it comes in, and let it drop into your belly. Notice, as you inhale, the rise of your belly. As you exhale, notice the release and the letting go. Let yourself breathe. Sit for five minutes and allow your body to relax. Keep the mind focused on the breath and mentally say to yourself, "I am breathing in" when you breathe in and "I am breathing out" when you breathe out.

Gratitude. To open up your heart, practice gratitude. Try this: make a list of everything you are grateful for about your body. Think about what it takes to walk, digest your food, see, hear, or touch something. Think about your internal organs and how they perform without your conscious input. Reflect on things that you may take for granted, hair, skin that is free from irritation, the ability to taste or chew. When your heart is open, you open up your perceptions and will see things in a new way. Stuck? Think of the people you love and what they bring to your life; then imagine life without them. Write down the things you love and are grateful for with your friends or family.

Be Generous. What can you do to bring benefit to someone else today? How can you contribute to another's well-being? Try a random act of kindness or the penny meditation. Pennies are good luck, and I know when I find one I always feel like I am in the right place. Throw some pennies and send good luck out to others. This one sounds so corny, but it works. As you throw a penny on the ground, think of someone coming along and finding it. What might be going on in their life? Maybe they are struggling or feeling a bit lost. I have used this exercise when I have been over focused on my challenges. I have found it to be fun, playful, and I really enjoy it. My kids laugh when they hear pennies hitting the ground, but they are used to it now and know I'm sending good luck out into the world. But the real gift is that it opens up my heart and let's my perspective shift.

Lighten up! You know you are attached and in control (not in trust) when you are taking everything very seriously. Whether you are concerned about yourself or your situation, losing your sense of humor will cause you to lose spaciousness and, therefore, the opportunity to open up to what is possible.

Find the humor! Nothing creates space faster or more efficiently than a good laugh. Physiologically, it contracts and relaxes the muscles of the diaphragm, thorax, abdomen, heart, and lungs and gives your body a good workout. It even boosts your immune system by reducing the stress hormone cortisol. It also creates space in the mind. Regardless of how intense I may be feeling about something or how much I've stressed myself out, if I hear a remark that makes me laugh, I lighten up. All of a sudden things don't seem so vitally important, and I see a new perspective.

It's been said that we see what we love. Comedians love humor. They see it everywhere, and it's their sharing of the most mundane aspects of life, seen through their lens, that lets us find the humor as well. Finding or not finding humor can let us know when we are attached and taking things too seriously, including ourselves. Life can be softhearted, and even more so when we can laugh at our own foibles.

Play. Life is so short. Don't miss a moment of it or put off your happiness a minute more. You can adapt an attitude of playfulness and optimism, regardless of what you are doing. Here are some ways to become more optimistic:

Anticipate that the unexpected could happen. Even if you plan out everything you can think of, most things don't work out 100%. If they do, be grateful! But if they don't, look at it as an opportunity to practice your problem solving skills.

Accept things as they are. If you are short, you will always be short, no matter how much you'd like to be tall. The more you focus on being tall, the more you will agonize.

Why agonize? Accept it and move on.

Sometimes a word puzzle or game is exactly what you need. They provide a terrific way to redirect your attention and let your mind rest.

Find meaning. Live your life with meaning. Know the direction and purpose of your life. Take the time to discover who you are and learn more about what you are to share with the rest of us. Ask yourself the tough questions. Who am I? What am I here for? What do I believe in? Where do I fill up? Or as Einstein said, "Is the universe a friendly place or not?"

Clear out. The Chinese art of Feng Shui is about working with our surroundings to clear out and arrange furniture and accessories in such a way that it frees up energy. Clutter around us translates to clutter within. Look at your surroundings to make sure that they support your desire for spaciousness.

The more we let go of in our lives, the more life can come in. Most of us have a lot of stuff. Having more than we need limits space in our life. After clearing out her closet and taking six bags of clothes to Goodwill, my client said, "Looking in my closet, it's like the first time ever that there has been space between my clothes. It's like they can finally breathe!" Look around your house, office, or car. What can you clear out? What can you give away to others who may have a need? Do it now, and free some space up for yourself. Notice what happens and how you feel.

Fix your gaze on something or someone. Now soften your eyes. If it's hard for you to feel the shift with this practice, think of something you love. When we think of something we love, we automatically soften our eyes. Stay focused with soft eyes for five minutes, then gently close your eyes and be still. When we soften our gaze, we mentally let go of what we are holding onto so tightly as well. This creates space both mentally and physically.

Find beauty. Make it a point to seek out beauty. What is beautiful for you? Beauty can be found everywhere. Look at your surroundings or find scenes in nature or elsewhere that fill your heart.

Practice forgiveness. Forgiveness begins with the intention of letting go. It's incredibly painful to think of doing this when you have been hurt, and it is not easy. But the great teachers and spiritual leaders remind us that when we hold a grudge we keep ourselves from being free. Is there someone or something in your life that you need to forgive? One way to know how much energy is being used to hold on to anger or resentment is to gauge the "charge" you feel when the person, event, or circumstance is brought up. What do you feel? Does your body tighten or your throat constrict? Do you feel tearful or angry? If your body reacts, you probably still have energy tied up and would benefit from practicing forgiveness.

Here is an exercise to use to practice forgiveness. You can either do this with another or visualize the person in front of you as you go through the steps.

There are three parts; Forgiveness of the other person, asking for their forgiveness, and forgiving yourself.

Take some time to center and quiet yourself. Create a sacred space for this ritual by lighting a candle and making sure that you are not interrupted or rushed.

You to the other. (Name of the person)_____ I forgive you for anything you have done that in any way caused me hurt, pain, or suffering. I let go of any resentment I have toward you.

(Name of the person)_____, I ask you to forgive me for anything I have done that in any way caused you hurt, pain, or suffering. I am sorry and hope that you will be free of any resentment.

I (Your name)_____ forgive myself for anything I did that in any way caused myself or another hurt, pain, or suffering. I release any resentment and choose to be free and clear of anything that may hold me to this past hurt.

Take some time to sit quietly when you are finished. When you are ready take some time to write out any impressions or experiences you had.

Practices for Awareness

The obstacle for awareness is judgment. These practices encourage curiosity and openness in order to gain insights.

Feeling what is. This process for feeling is very effective and best done with a trusted friend. It's a powerful way to release emotions. Set aside at least thirty minutes for this ancient practice.

First, connect with your breath. Think of a time when you felt a strong emotion. Let it come up. When you feel a tightening or constriction in your body, stop, take a breath, and draw your attention to that place. Focus on the deepest level of feelings that you can identify. Pretend that you can see this constriction, ache, tightness, or sharp pain, and describe it to your friend or write it down. What does it look like? What is its shape, color, texture? Describe it in as much detail as you can, and then come back to your breath.

A simple and effective practice is to "Let the thoughts go; let the feelings be." Based on mindfulness teachings, this allows an individual to stay present while feeling. It's simply a matter of first noticing an emotion as it arises. Observe and find where you feel it in your body. See if you can locate it in one spot. Say to yourself, "Let the thoughts go; let the feelings be." Let this be a mantra that you repeat; then go back and continue to witness your feelings.

What did you discover? Did you find that the emotion changed shape or color? Did it move? Did you find it hard to let go of your thinking? If you did, you're not alone. What if you recognized the feeling, even described it, and yet it appeared to stay the same? If this happened for you, draw your attention down to the soles of your feet and then mentally scan up your body for any tightness or tension. Move from your feet to the top of your head and then go back and "see" the original area of constriction. Notice if there are any changes now. Pay attention to the color or shape. Sometimes, stepping back and scanning the body allows the shift. Deepen this skill with practice, and it will help you to develop a new relationship with your feelings. Rather than ignore or deny them, you'll find a rich source of information.

Releasing Breath. Stand up with your feet solid on the ground and your hands by your side. Think about whatever it is that is annoying you or causing anger. Visualize it as being arms length above your head. Now, take an inhaling breath and reach both hands up. When your arms are fully extended, visualize taking hold of whatever it is that is bothering you and grabbing it with your hands. Make a fist with both hands, as if they each contained your frustration.

As you exhale, bring your hands down and symbolically release what was in your hands into the earth. As you release, exhale your breath using your voice. Say "Ha!" loudly—the louder, the better. Bend your knees to protect your back as you throw your frustrations down on the ground. Do this three times, and then just stand with your eyes closed and your hands by your side. Breathe deeply from your abdomen.

Enhancing Emotional Awareness. Did you know that there are certain places in the body where emotions are found? Do you know where fear is held in the body? (The belly). How about anger? (Shoulders, neck.) It's important to recognize and call emotions by their correct names. To help increase awareness of your emotions, try the five-step process as outlined below. Practice this often, and you will find yourself more relaxed with the ability to let the emotions flow through you rather than becoming stuck and tight.

1. Where do I feel something happening in the body? Shoulders? Stomach? Head? Neck? Back? Temples? Heart?

2. What do I feel? Tightness? Constriction? Butterflies? Pain? Throbbing? Soreness?

3. Name it. Is it anger? Fear? Confusion? Sorrow? Sadness?

4. Place your hand wherever you feel the discomfort, name it, and then ask, "What am I _____ about? For example, if you felt tightness in the belly, ask "What am I fearful about?"

5. Breathe. Drop the breath into the belly and inhale and exhale through the nose. Allow yourself to be present and listen. Practice curiosity and stay open. Continue to breathe and be present with your body as you get information or until the discomfort subsides.

Emotional Record-Keeping. For one week, keep a record of your awareness of pleasant and unpleasant events. Each day, answer these questions:

1. What happened?

2. Were you aware of your feelings while this was happening?

3. What did you feel in your body?

When the week is up, look over your answers and open up to insights. What did you discover about yourself? What were most of your feelings? How did you release the tension or otherwise manage the emotions?

Practice Yoga. Take a yoga class. The intention of yoga is to bring the mind, heart, and body together with the breath. Yoga was originally developed to help quiet the mind for mediation by releasing constrictions in the body that cause distractions or discomfort. In fact, the word "yoga" means to yoke or join together. There are many videotapes and DVDs available and classes everywhere. You need very little to begin. I suggest if you haven't taken an introductory class, do. It will familiarize you with the language and introduce you to the basic poses.

Open-Ended Questions. Read through the following list of questions. If some jump out at you, take a sheet of paper and write the question down. Let yourself have plenty of time to let the answers come to you. It may happen quickly, or it may be a few weeks before you begin to get insights. Let go and trust the process.

- What is it that, when you are doing it, causes you to lose all sense of time?

- What is trying to happen right now in your life?

- What would you do if you had unlimited money and resources?

- Who would you like to spend a day with if it could be anyone?

- What is something that you would like to do if you knew you could not fail?

- What is getting in the way of being who you are?

- What do you know to be true?

- What is the quality of your faith when you cannot see what is unfolding?

- For you, what are the laws of life?

Dreams. Pay attention to your dreams. Before you go to bed at night, put a pencil and paper next to your bed. Create the intention that you will remember your dreams when you awaken. As soon as you wake up, write down anything you remember. The more you practice this, the more you will remember your dreams. Dreams are a rich source of information. There are a lot of books available on dream interpretation. I like to write down the dream, along with the feelings I had, upon waking. Remember the final answer always lies inside, so if you read or hear something from someone that doesn't ring true for you, trust yourself. Sometimes it takes a few days or longer for a dream to become clear.

Remember Your Young Self. Find a photo of yourself when you were small, five to eight years old or so. What did you love to do? What made you happy? Sad? What made you feel like you belonged? Write about this younger you. Ask others who knew you then their impressions of you at that age. What did you discover?

Signs and Signals. Pay attention to synchronicity, serendipity, and accidental happenings. Begin your day wondering what will surprise you during the next twenty-four hours. Put a question or request out and keep a log of the synchronicities that you begin to notice. Fight the temptation to ignore them or pretend they are meaningless. At the end of the day, ask yourself what surprised you, what brought you joy or pleasure, and what you learned.

Eat Mindfully. Practice being present by having a mindful meal. Give yourself plenty of time and eat very slowly, paying attention to each bite. Start by looking at your plate and waiting a full minute before eating. Then slowly eat only one-fourth of the meal. Put your fork down and wait for three minutes before eating the next one-fourth of your meal. Once again put your fork down and wait three minutes. Then eat the next one-fourth; wait again for three minutes and finish the rest of the meal. When you are done, put your fork down and sit quietly for three minutes before getting up. Be present to the tastes, sensations, and aromas of the food you're eating. What did you discover? How did your food taste?

Have a Massage. Get a full body massage. If you haven't had one before, it's well worth the cost. Not only does it relax you, but it's also beneficial for your immune system. If a full body massage seems like too much, try reflexology—a foot massage. Touch is a powerful gift for well-being when done in a respectful and nurturing environment.

Do Something New. Get out of your comfort zone and experiment. Even if it's taking a new route on the way home from work . . . expand! Creativity thrives with newness. The more we experiment, the more creative we become. Welcome change every day, and open yourself up to its gifts of fun, playfulness, and surprise.

- Shop for clothes and buy a color that you normally don't buy.

- Call someone you haven't spoken to in years to check in on them.

- Take a comedy class.

- Go to an ethnic restaurant, one that you know nothing about.

- Take an art class.

- Play chess at a public park on the outdoor tables.

- Take up a new language.

Ask and Answer. As a way to listen to your inner voice, write out your own questions on a legal pad and then answer them without editing. Simply write down whatever comes up. You may want to write the questions with your dominant hand and answer them with your non-dominant hand. Or do this: Write your question in an e-mail and send it to yourself. Wait twenty-four hours before opening it. By the time you open that message, you may find that you already know the answer.

the art & practice of trust

Practices for Discernment

The practices for discernment are to encourage decision making, release fear, build self trust, and gain clarity.

Write your vision. Take some time to think about each of the following areas. List three to five things that you would like to achieve in each area and write them down. Try to project a year from now, or even five to ten years down the road.

- Health   _____ _____ _____
- Partner/Relationship _____ _____ _____
- Family   _____ _____ _____
- Friends   _____ _____ _____
- Work   _____ _____ _____
- Financial   _____ _____ _____
- Home   _____ _____ _____
- Adventure   _____ _____ _____
- Learning   _____ _____ _____
- Hobbies   _____ _____ _____

Your vision is your view of the desirable and achievable future that you want. Ideally, it stretches you out of your comfort zone, taking you beyond where you are at this moment. As Albert Einstein said, "...imagination is more important than knowledge. For knowledge is limited, whereas imagination embraces the entire world, stimulating progress, giving birth to evolution."

Using the ideas you uncovered and the headings as a guide, write out more fully what you want in each of these areas. Delve into your imagination. Daydream, reflect, doodle, and let your dreams for your life unfold. Take all the time you need. This process might take a few days, a month, or even a year. Just let it unfold. Simply focus on what you most want to create and on what is most important to you. Feel these things as you write them down and let yourself "be" in the future you are creating.

When you feel or sense that you have written down everything you want to create in your life, write a brief vision statement that sums it up. To do this, craft a sentence or short paragraph that includes the items you have just written down and that:

- Speaks to you and your heart

- Motivates and inspires you

- Is achievable, not a fantasy

- Fits with your values

- Is bigger than your own perceived limits

- Is empowering and an exciting reason for living

Write your vision statement here:

_____

_____

_____

_____

In addition to a written vision statement or as an alternative to writing one, you could make a collage to illustrate your vision and dreams. Each January I take some time to create a collage for the year. Cutting out images and words from my favorite magazines, I lay the collage out on a colored poster board, and when I'm finished, I hang it somewhere visible. It thrills and inspires me each time I look at it. And it draws me forward, into life rather than back into the past. Create something that is meaningful for you and that draws you forward. Let your vision inspire you.

Your Values. What do you stand for? What do you believe in? How do you want to live? Values are our hidden motivators. They initiate and drive our behaviors. These abstract principles guide our decision-making and provide the "rules of the game" in our life story. In short, values tell us why we do the things we do, and our observable behavior is a reflection of our values.

Take a moment to reflect on your values. Here are a few examples of some commonly recognized ones. Put a check by all those that you care deeply about and add your own at the end of the list. Check the ones that are so important to you that you would let go of a business or personal relationship if these values were lacking. It's easy to put checks by all of them because they are generally perceived as important but really take the time to listen and reflect.

___	Making a difference	___	Building wealth
___	Competition	___	Health
___	Intellectual Status	___	Stability
___	Forgiveness	___	Consensus
___	Appearance	___	Environment
___	Teamwork	___	Belonging
___	Authority	___	Security
___	Prosperity	___	Fairness
___	Power	___	Integrity
___	Responsibility	___	Family
___	Intimacy	___	Love
___	Achievement	___	Service
___	Adventure	___	Self-actualization
___	Happiness	___	Trust
___	Peace of mind	___	Accomplishment
___	Peace	___	Recognition
___	Patience	___	Faith
___	Determination	___	Perseverance
___	Creativity	___	Commitment to growth

Now, select and narrow that list down to your top ten values. Give yourself plenty of time to think about it and weigh the importance of each value in your life. Once you're certain, write them on a separate sheet of paper and label them personal values.

Can you think of times when you used your personal

values to make difficult decisions? What about when you didn't follow your values? How did that feel? How about your friends? Do they share your values? How about your workplace colleagues? If your friends saw the list of core values, would they recognize them as yours? If not, why not? Take a moment to reflect on these questions and write out your answers.

When we speak and live according to our personal values, it is obvious to everyone around us. Others see us fully through our actions. I once heard a quote, "Who you are is speaking so loudly, I can't hear what you are saying." The way we live our values tells people who we are without our having to say a word.

Discerning personal values is not something to be done once in our lives and then simply forgotten about. Values change as we grow and change. Your values at age twenty may be very different from your values at fifty. Revisit your values often to make sure that they remain meaningful and current.

Meditate or practice contemplative prayer. The fastest route to connecting with your inner wisdom is to show up and listen. Don't be concerned about starting with ten or twenty minutes—start with five. Even that amount, consistently done every day, will help you to feel a shift that will encourage you to do more.

Find a quiet place, set a timer, and begin. Stay connected with your breath or a mantra. Some popular ones are: "Be still and know that I am God," "Om," "Shanti," "Love, Peace, Be happy"; but your mantra can be any word or phrase that brings stillness and comfort to you. The idea is simply to quiet your mind, be present, and connect with the Source of Life.

Mindful walking is done by being fully present during the practice of walking. Stand up and connect with your breathing. Slowly lift your left foot; as you place your heel down, feel the shift and sensation along the bottom of your foot as your full weight is placed on it. Pay attention to shifting your full weight on your left foot; then slowly lift your right foot. Feel the pressure and each sensation on the bottom of your feet. Notice the temperature, the colors, and the objects that surround you as you walk. Stay connected with your breathing, and stay present to the moment.

Write in the a.m. One of the best tools I know for dissipating fear and connecting with your own voice of inner wisdom is through writing. First thing in the morning, simply write whatever is in your mind, letting it flow without censuring yourself. Make sure that the pages stay private so that you can be completely honest. Once written, just put them away to review at another time if you so wish. Let the time that you spend writing be one of freedom to really express your emotions and thoughts. After a while, you will discover a very wise part of yourself. In some traditions, this is called being "the observer." This wise voice is your inner wisdom, and the more you write the stronger that voice will become. The process can be done anytime you need it, but like all practices, doing them when things are calm will make them easier to call on when things get tough. To learn more I recommend, <u>The Artist Way</u>, by Julia Cameron.

Energy Testing. Find someone to work with, and have that person extend an arm straight out. To establish what a positive or a negative response feels like, have the person begin to think about personal worries or concerns. Let the person dwell on these worries for a few seconds, and then ask him or her to resist the pressure that you are about to apply. Take one of your hands, place it on the person's extended wrist, and push down. Tell them to resist. Notice what happens. Now repeat the experiment, but this time ask the person with the extended arm to think of something or someone loved. Ask the person to really feel the object of love, to see it, and sense it. Again, take your hand and press down on his or her wrist. What did you notice?

Usually when people are thinking about love, their extended arms are much stronger. I remember the first time I did this with an athlete. This man was the CFO of a mid-size business and a tri-athlete. When his arm tested strong when thinking of love and weak when he worried, he said with a quizzical expression, "I thought when I thought about love my arm would be weak." He was genuinely surprised to discover that the feeling of love strengthened rather than weakened him.

Walk a labyrinth. Labyrinths, contemplative tools that have been around for more than 4,000 years, have experienced a renaissance in the last ten to fifteen years. The unique circular design of labyrinths is found in many cultures. With their newfound popularity, labyrinths now can be found in churches, retreat centers, or parks in many cities. A labyrinth is a twisting path that has only one way in and out and is a physical representation of life. As you walk it through all the curves, turns, and twists, you can reflect on the experiences, changes, and challenges of your own life. At the labyrinth's center is space to stop, think, and be still. This space can represent heaven, God, a personal goal, or self-discovery.

Before you start to walk a labyrinth, be still and create a question or intention for your walk. Then begin. Notice your thoughts, feelings, and senses as you walk toward the center and then back out. Symbolically, entering a labyrinth represents going within one's self. Walking out symbolizes bringing what you have learned back out into the world. During times of transitions, change, and confusion, walking a labyrinth is a simple, peaceful way to reconnect with yourself and quiet your mind.

Explore your hidden values. Hidden values are values that you admire and respect in others but haven't quite taken on yourself—they are still "hidden" within you. It's good to recognize them, because then you can begin to incorporate them into your life.

Think of five people—alive, dead, known, or unknown to you—for whom you have great respect and admiration. They can even be fictional characters. Write those names down on a piece of paper. Next to each one, write down at least two (no more than four) qualities that the person embodies that you admire or respect.

Those values are your hidden values. They are values that you appreciate in others but may not have developed fully in yourself. Place a symbol of that value or write the word on pieces of paper posted in your home to trigger your consciousness of it—this practice will remind you to begin acting from that value yourself.

Practice a heart opening yoga pose of restoration. The practice of yoga is thousands of years old. It was originally developed to help quiet the mind for meditation by releasing constrictions in the body that caused discomfort and distraction. The poses that open the heart are those

Practices for Discernment

that bring the shoulder blades together. This extends the heart upward. These poses, by their very nature, invite vulnerability, yet also invite us into our hearts.

One such pose is called Supta Badha Konasana. It requires the use of three bath towels. Take two of the bath towels and fold them in half, laying one on top of the other. Roll them up to create a bolster. Sit on the floor with your legs extended and place the rolled-up towels behind you. Lay the bolster so that it lines up with your spine, and then lie back, allowing your spine to rest on the top of the bolster you've created. Take the third towel and create a support under your head so that your chin is level and your neck and head are supported. Let your arms lie on the ground by your sides. Close your eyes and drop your breath into your belly. If you are protecting your lower back, you can bend your knees while keeping your feet flat on the ground, or lengthen your legs and bring the soles of your feet together, letting your knees relax outward. Find the pose that works for you and rest here for five minutes. After five minutes, remove the towels and lie flat on the ground for another few minutes before getting up slowly.

Use symbols for discovery. Using symbols helps us discover what we know at a deep level but may not perceive in our conscious mind. Take a few minutes to set an intention or ask a question. Let it be open for example the question I often use is, "What's important now?" Get a basket or other container to place objects in. Hold the question you've chosen in your mind. Walk around in your house (or outside, or in the workplace) and when an object catches your eye, put it in the container. Continue until you feel you have enough objects. There is no right or wrong number. When finished, place the objects onto a clear space and move them until you feel they're in just the right location. When you're ready, talk about each one. Write down as specifically as you can (or have someone else write down) everything you say as you speak about each object. Say what it is that drew you to the object, what you liked or didn't like about it, and, if you don't know why you chose the object, just say that. Read your notes back to yourself or listen to your companion read them out loud, and then look for insights or meanings beyond the obvious. There is a reason you placed the objects as you did. Be a detective and observe. Always check in with your heart to make sure it resonates with what you're saying, and feel free to leave the arrangement up for a few days or a week. Sometimes it takes awhile to discover the elements that bring clarity.

Nature is a great and wise teacher. Throughout nature, there are many opportunities to observe how to relax and flow with life or deal with difficulties. For example, streams and creeks can demonstrate how to release and flow with life. Oceans are good examples of abundance. Fall leaves teach us about letting go, and mountains might represent strength or standing tall. Although there are symbols that have universal meanings, it really is an individual choice as to what each one means to you. Find an element in nature that inspires you and use the symbol to support your growth. Put it somewhere visible and use it as a reminder of the aspect it represents.

Call a clearing committee. Ask 4-6 close friends to meet with you for up to three hours to help you work through an issue you are grappling with. As this activity requires a high level of trust and confidence, choose people that you feel can participate fully with respect, trust, and honor. With you in the center of the circle, have them sit in front of you in a semi circle and begin with a prayer or intention. The idea is for them to only ask questions. No suggestions, no advice and no questioning your answers. This is a time for you to listen deeply from within as you answer questions. Establish ahead of time the importance of silence and of allowing only one person to speak at a time. As this is a sacred gathering, at the close give gratitude and let each person talk a few minutes about what this experience was like for him or her. This practice has been used for years in the Quaker Tradition, as they know that there is a deep wisdom and creativity available within groups when the trust is high.

Ask three questions. Once a year write out these three questions and answer them. Give yourself a week to complete this exercise so that you have plenty of time to reflect.

1. What is ending for me at this time in my life?

2. What is continuing on?

3. What is new that is coming in?

These are powerful questions. They tap right into what it is that we may know at an unconscious level and bring it up for us to see. Let your answers be spontaneous and write without editing. Once you have your finished list, see if there is anything on there that you need to explore further. Take your time. When it is complete, you may want to burn or tear up what is ending and place what is new somewhere that you can see it.

the art & practice of trust

Practices for Action

The practices for taking action are to help strengthen commitment, increase inner confidence and empower you to act.

Daily reminders. Print some or all of these daily reminders on index cards or post-it notes and read them to build confidence.

- Everything you watch or read goes into your mind and stays there on some level. Be selective and feed your mind ideas and images that help you to grow and feel good about who you are and the work you do.

- Place yourself well. Watch what you surround yourself with and allow into your life. Ask, how does this serve me?

- You can do what you perceive you can do. Pay attention to what you are thinking, and if you discover messages you don't want to live by, change them.

- Everything you pay attention to grows. Think of it as adding energy to thoughts, and remember that anything you add energy to will be attracted into your life.

- Opportunities can come up where you least expect them. Stay open to possibilities.

- Embrace uncertainty.

- Live your strengths, and listen to your heart.

- If you are passionate about something, follow it.

- Question assumptions.

- Add variety to your life. Shake up your routine and bring in creativity.

- If you want to make something happen, start making changes right now, even if those actions are very small and simple. Opportunities show up when you take action.

Uncover a limiting perception or an old tired story. Ask yourself this simple question: *How do I prevent myself from doing or being all that I could do or be?* Then, without analyzing it, write down what comes into your mind first. Spend about ten minutes writing. Trust that the most important things will come out. This exercise is not for the purpose of beating yourself up, but rather for receiving honest information about where you are holding back. Be gentle with yourself as you proceed with this exercise. You are on sacred ground. It takes a lot of courage to answer this truthfully.

Here are some examples of untruths and how some individuals held themselves back.

Don could never find the time to take care of himself and his own needs.

1. *How do I hold myself back?* "I say, 'I'm too busy. I don't have time to exercise or take care of myself.'"

2. *What do I say when talking to myself or others about this problem?* "There's too much to do. Other people

need me."

3. *What is at the core of this statement? What do I perceive to be true?* "Other people's needs are more important than mine."

Betty, a beautiful woman in her late 50s, mentioned often that when she was in her early 30s and 40s, she turned heads whenever she entered a room. "I am scared of getting older," she repeatedly said. "People become invisible when they get old."

Here's the process that Betty went through:

1. *How do I hold myself back?* "I'm afraid of getting older and not being useful."

2. *What do I say when talking to myself or others about this problem?* "If I'm older, others won't want to work with me and I'll be left out."

3. *At the core of this statement what do I perceive to be true?* "Aging equals being worthless."

Ever since she was little, Christine has been shy. She liked staying in the background because it seemed that when she did speak up or was receiving attention, criticism came along with it. In recent years she has become passionate about abandoned animals and wanted very much to speak out in their behalf. As a board member for the local animal shelter, she has been asked to speak at a fundraiser and wants to—but feels paralyzed at the thought of standing up in front of a group.

This was Christine's line of questioning:

1. *How do I hold myself back?* "I hide, stay in the background and play small. I don't speak out when I want to. I let others intimidate me."

2. *What do I say when talking to myself or others about this problem?* "Others will judge me and will hurt me."

3. *At the core of this statement what do I perceive to be true?* "I can't take care of myself—and maybe I won't survive."

As the statements above indicate, what is believed to be true is held at a very deep level; and there may be embarrassment, shame or fear when one discovers the core of the limiting belief. When that happens, know that you're right on course and continue. Once you clearly see the fallacy of the belief, you can choose to let it go and replace it with a new, empowering belief. To be effective, the empowering belief must bridge the heart and mind. It has to be felt on an emotional level in order to effect change, or else it's just a mental exercise. Therefore, the words that you choose for the new belief are very important. They have to speak directly to your heart. It doesn't matter what anyone else thinks or feels about the wording, what matters is how it resonates within you.

Don's empowering belief had to support the truth that he was important and his well-being was important. He chose "My well-being is important and I matter."

Betty realized that although physical beauty catches people's eyes, there is also a beauty that comes from a loving presence and service to others. She realized that although she was, according to society, "losing" the beauty of her youth, she still was beautiful within and without; and there were many ways to receive attention. The new vision that captured her heart was "I radiate warmth and beauty and am secure in my worth."

Christine learned that she could question criticism and would not die when others judged her. Her new, empowering belief became "I am enough and courageously step into my destiny."

Once you have your new belief, feed it. Read it every night before you go to bed and in the morning before you begin your day until you've absorbed it, and it's part of your truth. The minutes just before we go to bed and when we first awaken are when our conscious and subconscious are most aligned.

Make a balanced plan and be accountable. Making a plan and sharing it with others will help you to stay focused on what is most important. Keep it simple and balanced. Prioritize self-care, as well as the goals you wish to achieve. Set the time frame. What do you want to achieve over the next month, year, or five years? What is most important to accomplish? Make the list of the top 5-8 goals. Are you willing to set up accountability? Find a partner, a coach, and a good friend who will hold you accountable and help you creatively address any obstacles. Make sure that this partner empowers you and brings you back to your vision, your radical responsibility, and your commitment. Celebrate your successes! Each time you achieve a goal, recognize the effort and work that went into it. When you do, you will pick up extra energy and that will help you produce more in the future.

Step out. On the date of your birth each month, do something outside of your comfort zone. Practice taking a risk and noticing what that feels like. If you do that each month, at the end of the year you will have done twelve things outside of your comfort zone.

Break free of perfectionism. Try these strategies if you need to break the habit of perfectionism.

- When you feel yourself trying to be perfect, slow down and reflect on how perfectionism separates us from others and causes undue stress. Aim instead for excellence. Remind yourself that, It does not have to be perfect to be great.

- Give yourself a deadline.

- Delegate. Let go of minutiae. If others can do the work faster or better, let them.

- Appreciate degrees of excellence. Sometimes a B+ is good enough.

- When you hear a critical voice, ask yourself whose voice that is. Usually it's the voice of someone from your past. Ignore it, and instead pay attention to individuals who can give you honest feedback.

Over the years, I have seen hundreds of people come up with limiting beliefs and old stories around the same five issues. They are:

1. I am not _____ enough. (Fill in the blank – pretty, rich, young, smart . . .)

2. I don't matter or my well-being is not important.

3. I am not deserving of _____ (Fill in the blank – love, good fortune, abundance, happiness . . .)

4. I can't trust_____ (Fill in the blank – myself, life, other people . . .)

5. There's not enough _____ to do what I want to do. (Fill in the blank – time, money, energy, resources, support . . .)

Do any of these feel familiar to you? Have you had similar thoughts? If so, what would your life be like without them? Take a minute and write about this and what is possible.

Focus on what is working. Each night, or at least once a week, make a list of everything you have accomplished. Take time to congratulate yourself and recognize all that you have done. So many times we forget to look at our achievements. Develop the habit of catching yourself doing well.

Serve others. Who can you help? How can you be of service? Service to others is a way to give back to life. Take time to volunteer, share, and help out where needed. Notice the way you feel after you have been of service to another. I remember times when I was feeling so down and was very self-absorbed. I would make myself do something for someone else, and it never failed to lift my spirits as well. All of the faith traditions encourage service because it not only serves a need for the other person, but it gets you out of yourself and that downward inner spiral of over reflection or judgment.

Chant. Performer Tina Turner chants every morning and credits it with keeping her life rich, full, and connected to her heart. Chanting is simply repeating a word, phrase, or mantra in song. The voice is a powerful medium, so singing or chanting opens not only our hearts, but also our throat chakra through which we bring our voice and our will out into the world. Chanting "Om," the universal sound of wholeness, opens all the chakras and literally massages you from inside out. Like a still pond when a rock is dropped into it, the chanting vibrations resonate and spread throughout our bodies. Practice singing or chanting and then sitting in silence. Allow yourself to be present and feel what wells up in the silence.

Make your dream real. Once you commit to something, put your attention on what you want to have happen. See yourself doing, having, or being whatever it is that you are committed to. Let it be as real as you can make it. Feel what it feels like to have accomplished it. This is not pretending or living in a dream, but instead using the power of your heart and mind to draw you forward. This will help to inspire you. There is a universal law of attraction that says what you focus on is drawn to you. Try it. Focus all your attention on what it would feel like to achieve what you want and then from that place choose to take one action that brings you closer to it.

Acknowledgments

A sincere offering of gratitude to my favorite authors, poet and teachers: Angeles Arrien, PhD, Joan Borysenko, PhD, Jean Houston, PhD, Steven Covey, PhD, David Whyte, and Laura Hillenbrand. Your books opened the door of my mind, spoke directly to my heart, and offered me new ways to think and live. I am forever grateful.

A big thank you to my clients and to the business teams that I have been privileged to work with. Thank you for your trust. I am inspired by your courage, integrity and willingness to grow.

Many thanks to Sara Valentine for the cover art, and Laureen Mauer for the cover layout.

To Theo Koffler, my precious friend, whose enormous capacity for loving kindness and service inspires me and whose love and support empowered this work.

To my dear friends for their endless generosity, love, and open arms; Tilli Williams, Mary Helen O'Keeffee, Karen Rapp, Ann Smith, Mary Zimmerman, Bonnie Coffey, Jane Marshall and Amy, Courtney and Casey Vogt. Also I offer love, appreciation and gratitude to Eric Ryan, Blake and Lisa Peterson, Laura Hughes and Diana Baysinger for their caring friendship. To the students, teachers and community of Desert Song Yoga and Massage Center for the joy, encouragement and inspiration so freely given. And great gratitude to John Friend, Meg Byerlein, Mary Beth Markus and Erich Schiffmann for their yoga teachings and offerings of the heart. To my friends, Dan Siegel, Bill Harrison and Mary Bruce for their loving friendship.

A big thank you to friends and colleagues Larry Spears, Kathy Orlay, Shelly Blackman, Robert Mines, PhD. and Nancy Stone for reading the manuscript and offering helpful feedback. Your advice and suggestions were of great help.

I also want to offer a sincere thank you to Gloria Wallace, Kathryn Hallsten, MD, Carol Levin, Rachel Remen, MD, and Marion Weber. Each one of you made a difference in my life through your teaching and/or friendship. Great appreciation to Jim Myers for his encouragement and wise leadership. Gratitude and love to Pastor Kelly Bender and the community of Paradise Valley United Methodist. A special thank you to David Bruno for his belief in me and seeing the value in this book.

With great love and joy I offer gratitude to my mom and dad, Jeannette and Stan Brown, my sisters Jan Moberg, Joan Brown, and Christie Lebling. As well as to my brothers Chip Brown and Bill Lebling, and my nieces and nephews Jenny, Pete Wintermute, Kim Brown, Kyle, Jeremy, and Jenna Lebling. And to our newest member, Miss Kinsley Wintermute.

And from my heart, a big hug and thank you to my children, Sarah, Brian and Jeff Crawford, for their love, encouragement and inspiration.

For Lucy, my writing buddy and forever dog who had me laughing each day.

An extra special thank you to Thich Nhat Hanh and H. H. Dalai Lama whose practices and efforts for peace inspire me daily.

Lastly and most importantly, I am grateful, humbled and blessed by the opportunity to write and share what I have learned with others. I thank God for the inspiration, guidance and the courage that made it possible.

Note: The stories in this book come from my personal life and from the lives of clients, family, and friends. Although permission has been given, names have been changed to protect privacy.

the art & practice of trust

About the Author

Victoria Crawford is a personal leadership coach, speaker and workshop leader committed to building trust and helping individuals, teams and organizations realize their greatest potential.

Since founding Way of Discovery in 1998, her client list has included management teams of Fortune 500 companies, small business leadership teams and individuals that want to navigate transitions, realize a vision or simply be at their best.

Victoria is a certified yoga instructor with thirteen years of experience. She bridges her knowledge of the heart, mind and body with practical tools and techniques to support balanced action and growth.

She lives in Phoenix, Arizona with her family and beloved dog, Lucy.

Please contact us at www.wayofdiscovery.com or 602-870-0060 for more information about personal leadership coaching, workshops, speaking and team development for yourself or your business. We welcome any comments or stories you may wish to share about how The Way of Discovery has helped make a difference for you, your work and your life!

References

Books

- Arrien, Angeles. *The Four Fold Way* (San Francisco, Harpers Collins Press, 1992)
- Borysenko, Joan. *Minding The Body, Mending The Mind* (Reading, Mass. Bantam Book, 1987)
- Casarjian, Robin. *Forgiveness, A Bold Choice for a Peaceful Heart* (New York, Bantam Books, 1992)
- Chodron, Pema. *Comfortable with Uncertainty* (Boston, Shambhala Press, 2003)
- Chodron, Pema. *The Wisdom of No Escape* (Boston and London, Shambhala Press, 2001)
- Cohen, Allen. *Wisdom of the Heart* (Carlsbad, Hay House, 2002)
- Cohen, Kenneth. *The Way of QiGong* (New York, Ballantine Books, 1997)
- Combs, Deidre. *The Way of Conflict* (Novato, New World Library, 2004)
- Covey, Steven. *The Seven Habits of Highly Effective People* (New York: Simon and Schuster Press, 1989).
- Covey, Steven M.R. *The Speed of Trust.* (New York: Free Press, 2006)
- Dass & Gorman, Ram and Paul. *How Can I Help?* (New York, Borzoi, 1985)
- Ditzler, Jinny. *Your Best Year Yet!* (Hammersmith, London, Thorsons, 1994)
- Friends of Peace Pilgrim. *Peace Pilgrim* (Hemet, California, Ocean Tree Books, 1982)
- Goleman, Daniel. *Primal Leadership* (Boston, Harvard Business School Publishing, 2002)

- Greenleaf, Robert. *Servant Leadership* (New Jersey, Paulist Press, 1977)
- Hanh, Thich Nhat . *Be Free Where You are* (Berkeley, California: Parallax Press, 2002)
- Hanh, Thich Nhat *The Miracle of Mindfulness* (Boston, Beacon Press, 1975)
- Hanh, Thich Nhat. *Peace Is Every Step* (New York, Bantam Books, 1991)
- Hawkins, David. *Power versus Force, The Hidden Determinants of Human Behavior* (Carlsbad, Hay House, 1995)
- Jeffers, Susan. *Feel the Fear and Do It Anyway!* (New York, Ballantine Books, 1987)
- Kabat-Zinn, Jon. *Wherever You Go There You Are* (New York, Hyperion, 1994)
- Katie, Byron. *Loving What Is* (New York, Three Rivers Press, 2002)
- Lama, His Holiness the Dalai. *A Simple Path* (Hammersmith, Harpers Collins, 2000)
- Nichols, Michael. *The Lost Art of Listening* (New York, Guilford Press, 1995)
- Muller, Wayne. *Sabbath, Restoring the Sacred Rhythm of Rest* (New York, Bantam Books, 1999)
- Palmer, Parker. *Let Your Life Speak* (San Francisco, Jossey-Bass Inc. 2000)
- Reina & Reina, Dennis and Michelle. *Trust and Betrayal in the Workplace* (San Francisco, Berrett-Koehler, Inc., 1999)
- Schiffmann, Erich. *Yoga, the Spirit and Practice of Moving into Stillness.* (Pocket Books,1996)
- Whyte, David. *Making a Friend of the Unknown.* (CD) (Many Rivers Company, Langley, WA. 1997)
- Whyte, David. *The Heart Aroused.* (New York, Currency Paperback, 1994)

Magazine Articles

Shambala Sun
    "This Floating World" by Joan Sutherland. March 2005
    "The Answer to Anger and Other Strong Emotion." by Pema Chodron. March 2005
    "The Man Who Prescribes the Medicine of the Moment." by Barry Boyce. May 2005

Shift
    "Molecules and Choice" by Candace Pert. November 2004

Yoga Journal
    "Hurts So Good" by Fred Mitouer. April 2000
    "The Well Spring of Joy" by Anne Cushman. February 2004

Ode
    "Peace is not a field of flowers. It's hard work." by Tijn Toube., June 2005

the art & practice of trust

www.ingramcontent.com/pod-product-compliance
Lightning Source LLC
Chambersburg PA
CBHW071719090426
42738CB00009B/1819